My Now for the Future Man

Todd,

Enjoy the Journey brother.

Live with a Courageous Heart.

S

Todd,

Enjoy the journey brother.

Live with a courageous Heart.

-J

My Now for the

Future Man

Moovin4ward Publishing
Huntsville, Alabama

Library of Congress Control Number: 2015919816

ISBN: Paperback 978-0-9910227-31

Printed in the United States of America

Publisher:

Moovin4ward Publishing
A Division of Moovin4ward Presentations LLC
www.Moovin4ward.com

Contents

My Now...

...for the *Future Man*

Mark W. Wiggins

Mark "The Speaker Man" Wiggins, an International speaker, trainer, author and entrepreneur is the CEO of Xtreme Effort Speaking. He has held leadership and management positions within several national retail companies, such as Foot Locker, Eddie Bauer, and Levi Strauss & Co. He has trained corporate, community, and association leaders in the Washington, DC area on the topics of customers, leadership and human performance.

He is the author of *Permission to Succeed: the Only Person Who Needs to Give it is You*; *MTXE the Formula for Success*; and more. He is also one of the featured authors of the book, *My Vision, My Plan, My NOW!*

Get my information right now! Text the word "Speakerman" to 90210
Email: Mark@markthespeakerman.com
Tweet: @Speakerman87

Awake

Mark Wiggins

Circa 1981

One day my father says, "Son, let's talk." I had to be about 14 years old, when my father said, "son there are some things I need to tell you, things that will help determine how successful you will be in your life, this will help you see things that you cannot see, and begin to learn how to navigate this thing called life. It is imperative that you hear this from me because, experience maybe the best teacher, but she gives the hardest tests."

The reason for the "father and son" talk occurred after, I had been in trouble at school, or that's what my school told my Dad. Growing up in Maple Heights, Ohio, the school system had decided to bus students from the east of Maple Heights to the west side of Maple Heights. So, I was bussed across the tracks to the predominately "white" side of town. I had attended school with other white students; however, these particular students on the west side of Maple Heights were very different. The white students on the west side of town had never attended school, nor interacted with black students, and many of the teachers in the school system did not have any experience with teaching students of another race outside of their own. So, the term "culture shock" went to another level. What lead to the discussion with my father was that there was another kid in the school named Marc Wiggins (another white student). I was shocked, a white dude with the same name, but spelled differently. White Marc, as we identified him was the opposite of me. This kid cut class, did drugs, and constantly in trouble all of the time. Me, I was the perfect child, right. So one day "Marc" got caught cutting class, and was sent to the office. However, instead of calling his parents, they called mine! Talk about a "mix-up." I had no idea of this situation because I was sitting in class minding my own business and doing my school work, and looking forward to football practice. Needless to say, when I got home that day I received a call from my mother saying, "You better stay up until your father gets home."

I still had no clue what my mother was talking about. She told me what happened, so I explained to her that it was not me, I had witnesses and the whole nine yards. Mom being Mom says that she was going to the school to get to the bottom of this. Not good for the school. Dad came home and gets the "debrief" from my mom, but he still seemed concerned and wanted to talk to me. I began to think which one of the branches off the maple tree in our back yard should I break off, the green branch or the older branch.

So, Pops comes to me and says, "we need to talk, there are some things I need to explain to you about life and not just being a young Black man, but about being a man into today's society, as a matter of fact, what I am about to share with you, you will have to share with your son and other young men that you come into contact with so pay attention."

Fast Forward 2013

My son's mother contacts me and says that our son, Marcellus, has experienced a few issues at his new school, but it appears that he is getting in more trouble that than other kids in his school. Déjà vu! My son attended a school that was very different from mine. It was a private school with students from a different socioeconomic background. These parents were taking their children on spring break vacations to wherever their jets could take them. However, it was similar to my school and experience because the racial mix was exactly the same. Much has changed, but not everything. Just as my father did, I told Marcellus' mother that I would look into it. (Have you ever felt that you were taking on the role of your parents?) I had a talk with my son to get his version of what happened at school. He told me about all the "situations" that were happening at the school. After listening to his saga, I knew exactly what had to be done. I needed to visit the school. Not so good for the school. I met with the administrator and she began to tell me about my son. Side note, I was not there when my parents went to the school, but I can imagine the conversation was sounding much like mine at the moment. My son's teacher said all of the right things; he is a good kid, one of the brightest in the school. But she emphasized that he needed to buckle down, etc. I needed to explain to the administrator, that she was preaching to the choir, and that they needed to see things from a different view point as it pertain to dealing with my son and other young black males that may come through these halls. More importantly, I realized it was now my time to share the same message my father shared with me. So, I told my son "we need to talk."

My Pops shared three life changing principles that I went on to share with my son and the youth that I work with. At some point in your life, you have to wake up to see what is going on around you, what is happening to you, and why. Then you have to have a plan. Without a plan, you often waste time and get distracted. And distractions lead to destruction. Persistence pays! It helps to develop habits and routines that make you more efficient, thus making you more productive. My pops kept it very real with me, helping me recognize the challenges that I already faced. He helped me see that I had to learn to better manage the things that I could control in life. The rest, Pops said, can be handled.

I like to sum these lessons up by telling young men that order to achieve their dreams and make better decisions, they need to be conscious, intentional, and consistent.

Conscious

When my dad spoke to me about being conscious, he referred to being aware of your surroundings. Understand the real layout of the land so that you will plan accordingly. When it comes to your friends, understand that you may or may not always be able to do what they are do, and get away with it. I have always been the comic one in the group. Needless to say, I spent a lot of time joking around, making people laugh. Sad to say, my friends were laughing at me, not with me. They were getting their work done and I was not. I needed to wake up. Being conscious means that you understand the forever action; there is an equal and opposite reaction. If you are not careful the reaction could be something that you did not intend. Play time is over! You need to focus on your goals and dreams and start to create a plan or a roadmap to your success. But in order to know where you want to go, you need to wake up and notice your own surroundings. Imagine a ship at sea with no power; it is just out there and going nowhere. Without power and direction it becomes subject to the wind, the waves, the current, and will be swiftly thrown off course. However, when the ship has power and uses the rudder to direct its course, the ship can navigate through the obstacles and reach its destination. It is the engaged power of the engine that allows this to happen. For you, you need to wake up and engage your mind so you can chart your course to success. Being conscious simply means, watching, listening, asking better questions, why instead of what, when instead of where, seeking out mentors involving yourself in programs that will help you get to where you go.

Intentional

Being intentional simply means, you have a purpose. In the world of motivational speaking, they say when you are presenting your movements should have purpose, they should be intentional. Your voice conveys your message, your passion and energy for your topic means something. This is how it should be when you gain consciousness and begin to plan for your success. Think about when you are focused on that video game or that new tech item you wanted, and when you get it, you spent countless hours on mastering that game. You died like 1.5 million times but you would not quit until you succeeded. That is intentionality. You must take the same approach to what you want in your life. It's about getting what you want, however you must first wake up and realize that you have dreams and goals. So how do you get that focus? First, find out what you are passionate about, because passion for your purpose will give you the strength to endure to the finish. Whatever the intentional thing is, that thing should motivate you to complete it, and when complete your task or reach your goal, you can say "I meant to do that." Here is a thought that I leave with my young basketball players that I train. "Whatever you won't do, someone will do, and when that person meets you they will beat you." Success is predictable, it can be planned for and it can be duplicated but you must be intentional about your success as you prepare for the opportunity.

"When preparation meets opportunity, success is born"

The Speaker Man

Consistent

When I was growing up, my dad was the motivator. Most likely, my father's influence is why I do what I do now. My father would come up with these cornball sayings like, 'if you can reach your goals with a step ladder then they are probably too low.' Really? He also had this definition for our last name, similar to a vision statement. *"Wiggins, means perpetual motion always on the go, striving to move ahead."* It took many years of repeating, and saying this phrase before I gained enough wisdom to figure out what my father was saying about our name and our purpose, or should I say my purpose. This statement all boils down to being consistent. Can you start something and have the tenacity to stick with it until it is done? Can you overcome your own shortcomings and limitations to find a workable solution to get to your goals? Consistent means you are working while others are sleeping, never giving up on your dream no matter how long it takes. Rapper and Actor LL Cool J. has been quoted to say, "**Success does not have an expiration date**." Being consistent is like the old argument of which is greater: the immoveable object or the unstoppable force. Something has to give. In both cases, both forces will remain consistent in their position, maintaining or even increasing pressure until something happens. You need to change your habits to support your new mentality geared toward success. It's not hard! Just start wherever you are. Wake up! Have your plan, work your plan, and don't stop until you succeed. Remember! Be conscious, intentional, and consistent!

Let me leave you with one final thought:

Success is not one major event. It's a series of small victories and achievements that elevate you to your goal. If you add these three simple things to your success tool box, you will be better prepared to have the success you desire. Remember! Be conscious, intentional, and consistent!

In case you never call my phone, here is my voice mail message: "If you can reach your goals with a step ladder, then they are probably too low!"

Thanks Pops for talking to me.

#getoffthebench

Kevin E. Boston-Hill

Kevin E. Boston-Hill is the consummate educator. He has been an educator at many levels in New York for over 18 years. He has conducted professional development workshops for his staff, families and others in many areas including instructional technology and 21st century learning. His profession gives him instant motivational opportunities, as he is a sought after speaker and emcee, having spoken to thousands of students from around the country.

As a member of Kappa Alpha Psi Fraternity, Inc., Kevin serves as the Northeastern Province (Regional) Guide Right Director. He coordinates activities, trainings, and conferences for all of the guide right programs and directors from Rhode Island to Delaware.

Kevin is also a voice actor and has recorded several audio and video projects that were used for professional development and training purposes. Kevin uses his experiences as an official in baseball/softball, basketball, and volleyball to further connect with and motivate the people he comes in contact with.

You can follow Kevin on Twitter (@kbhspeaks)
LinkedIn (www.linkedin.com/kbhspeaks)

Figuring Out the Puzzle That is YOU

Kevin E. Boston-Hill

"The difference between men and boys are the lessons they learn." ~ Biker Boyz

An author by the name of Robert Fulghum once wrote a poem and published a collection of short stories under the same title. The title was, "All I really need to know I learned in kindergarten". I encourage you to look it up as it does have some very practical information for you to remember as you get older. Of course, this is not an exhaustive list, but it is a good start.

I am sure that you have heard that life is a game and those who are successful at it learn the rules early on. However, as you may have also learned, the rules are always changing so how can you truly be successful at it? Instead of trying to master the things that are out of your control, concentrate on perfecting the one thing that you do have complete control of – yourself. Think of yourself as a puzzle that needs to be completed. Each piece of this puzzle, no matter how small or irregular, plays an important part in developing the man you will become. You need each of those pieces or else the picture of what you are to become will be incomplete and you will not be as equipped to deal with all that life has to throw at you. It is important to note that life is 10% what happens to you and 90% of how you react to it.

Think of each piece as an experience that will allow you to deal with similar circumstances that will follow. You do not know when this information will become handy, but rest assured that every experience has a reason and a purpose – be sure to make your choices wisely. However, even if you do make the occasional poor choice, find the lesson that should be learned and file the experience for later use. A line from a Billy Joel song (Google him) states, "Mistakes are the only things we can truly call our own". Make the mistake, learn from it, and never repeat it. This is part of the formula for maturity.

All of the pieces of the puzzle that makes who you are can be classified into five categories. These categories, which spell the acronym K.A.P.P.A., represent the tools you will need to develop to become successful. The qualities of Knowledge, Awareness, Perseverance, Preparation, and Achievement will go a long way to developing the man you are destined to become. The more attention you place on these qualities, the more complete your puzzle will become.

You have undoubtedly heard the phrase, "Knowledge is Power!" It may seem cliché, but it is an important statement. The more knowledge you have, the more doors you can open and the more options become available to you. In my youth, I did things that typical adolescents do – sports, hanging with friends, and getting into trouble...occasionally. One of those "occasions" occurred at the beginning of summer vacation. It has been so long that I do not remember exactly what I did, but needless to say it was serious enough to warrant that I be grounded for the ENTIRE SUMMER. Since this was a time before X-Box or PS3 or whatever the latest game system is, the only source of recreation for children was to be outside and now I had that taken away from me – for the ENTIRE SUMMER! As if this wasn't enough of a punishment, my father decided that I was not going to sit in the house watching TV all summer either, so he had me read every volume of Childcraft Books. These were a supplement of the World Book Encyclopedia. There were 15 volumes of this book series and I was instructed to read each and every one of them, or suffer additional consequences of the physically painful kind. You see, what is considered abuse today was simply a good old belt whoopin' in my youth.

In any event, I could not understand then why I needed to read every volume and subject myself to an oral examination of each. This was one of those irregular shapes that I had to somehow fit into my overall picture. Mind you, it was a piece that I had to hold onto for years before I realized its effectiveness. The ***knowledge*** I received from those books (a variety of poems, short stories, myths and fables from foreign lands, different types of animals and machinery) helped to provide the foundation and experience necessary for me to perform well on standardized exams (SAT for college, LSAT for law school) and to develop the reasoning ability to carry on conversations in a variety of settings. Something else happened as a result of reading all of those books – I developed a love of knowledge. After high school, I committed myself to being a lifelong learner – pursuing advanced degrees and participating in numerous professional and personal development opportunities. This knowledge has also allowed me to be selected for and perform well in interviews to obtain positions that would not have been available to me otherwise. While the initial event was deemed by me at the time to be cruel and unusual punishment, I am thankful that I was able to obtain a level of knowledge that I would not have received otherwise. That strangely shaped piece now fits perfectly, the way it was meant to.

Part of Fulghum's poem states, "When you go out into the world, watch out for traffic, hold hands, and stick together." Basically, you need to be ***aware*** of your surroundings and don't be afraid to ask for help to reach your goals. It is important to not go blindly into situations, or else it could cause more problems than you need to worry about. This is when you need to develop your "Spidey sense". We all have it. We just call it by another name – intuition or gut feeling. Most of the time when we get that feeling, we simply ignore it only to say to ourselves later on that, "I should have listened to myself" or "I knew I should have done that differently". The trick is to listen to your intuition when it initially becomes activated.

One afternoon I was conducting one of my regular patrols as assistant principal of the school where I worked – making sure the halls were clear of students, making sure those who were in the halls had proper passes, etc – when my "spidey sense" began tingling. I was drawn to the exit that leads to the parking lot. I went outside and some people walking by got my attention and pointed to the building behind me. I looked up at the school and noticed black smoke billowing out of what looked to be a classroom window. I ran back inside and raced to the fourth floor where the smoke was coming from. Along the way, I used my 2-way radio to alert school safety of the situation. A couple of agents met me on the fourth floor and immediately called 911 and pulled the fire alarm to evacuate the building. Three schools shared space in the building, but we were able to evacuate everyone in less than three minutes.

Once the fire department showed up, they were able to contain the fire to the office where it started. The damage, fortunately, was also isolated to that room. We were lucky that the fire (which originated in an outlet that had too many objects plugged into it) did not spread to the adjacent classrooms, which were full of students. Everyone evacuated the building safely and we were able to resume classes the following day. Thankfully we were able to address the situation before it got out of hand. If my "spidey sense" hadn't gone off, I wouldn't have walked outside and I wouldn't have been alerted to the smoke condition – which, strangely enough, no one else in the building detected or did anything about. In fact, most people were unaware of what was happening until the fire department showed up – including people on the fourth floor!

There are many other examples that could be used to show the benefit of having this "spidey sense". What needs to be understood is that this is not some superhuman sense that is bestowed upon us by some freak accident or genetic mutation. Instead it is a heightened awareness that occurs when all of our senses work together. This acuteness takes time, but it can be accomplished. It means truly observing your surroundings and the actions of those around you. You must be able to read any situation, including the potential consequences of your actions. This is especially important to remember when it comes to your interactions with women. You MUST recognize that a situation is becoming volatile and know how to walk away. No matter what she does and how you may feel, you will ALWAYS be in the wrong if you strike a female. This is one of the most unfair situations in life, but you must know this and follow it to the letter: *The second you strike a female, nothing that took place before that moment will matter. You WILL be the one to suffer any consequences.*

This means your ***awareness*** must be at the level it is when you are walking through an unfamiliar neighborhood by yourself at night. This is not to say you should operate from a position of fear, but you should be acutely aware – you need to practice the skill of complete observation. Always "watch out for traffic" – those situations and events that pop up in our paths from time to time. You can either listen to your intuition and avoid the traffic or ignore your gut and get run over like a game of Frogger (Google it).

Ralph Waldo Emerson once said, "What lies behind us and what lies before us are tiny matters compared to what lies within us". He was reminding us that ***perseverance*** is a key ingredient in creating the picture of who we are and who we will become. Perseverance can be summed up in a four-letter word: grit. According to Webster's dictionary, grit is a firmness of mind or spirit; unyielding courage in the face of hardship or danger. However, I believe G.R.I.T. is its own acronym – Greatness Revealed In Time. When you put it in terms of the puzzle that is you, it takes time to determine what the final image will be (remember, you don't have a box cover to look at – you are putting this puzzle together blindly). Don't rush into decisions and don't shy away from the work associated with a given situation. It is the work and the time you take that will help shape the person you will become. When I ran track I often found the practices to be quite grueling, especially when it came to running hills and stairs in the summer heat.

Training became especially difficult when I developed a stitch in my side or my legs were sore from the previous day's workout. As difficult and painful as it was, I knew I had to persevere and work through it. As a result of my mental toughness, I earned my fair share of medals and hold a few records at my high school. Obviously success did not happen overnight. It took time, but my greatness was eventually revealed. Always remember that just when you feel you can't go on any further, keep pushing, your greatness is about to be revealed. Harriett Beecher Stowe once said, "When you get into a tight place and everything goes against you, till it seems as though you could not hang on a minute longer, never give up then, for that is just the place and time that the tide will turn."

You may have heard the saying that luck favors the prepared. It is true that you can make your own luck and create your own opportunities. It all depends on your level of ***preparation***. I am sure you have had teachers and parents constantly remind you to do your homework. You may have even heard that phrase, "do your homework", in a different setting. Whatever the situation, the meaning and purpose is the same – you must do what you can to prepare yourself before entering any situation. You will soon be in a situation where you will be interviewing – whether it is for a job or admission to a school or program. You must remember to "do your homework". This means doing research to find out as much as you can about the company. This will enable you to determine how good a fit you will truly be and what benefit you will be to the company. This level of preparation will not only allow you to provide complete answers to any of their questions, but to interview them and ask questions. Many times, the questions you ask provide additional insight to the interviewer into who you are and what you will bring to their company. On the flip side, if you do not ask questions, you will also provide insight, though not necessarily favorable.

When you play a sport, you constantly have to be prepared or do your homework. In the off-season you spend time in the gym getting stronger and working on skills to get better. In the pre-season you review notes and tape of the previous year and get new information to incorporate. During the season, you scout opponents and locations to ***prepare*** as best you can and try to gain any edge you can. In the end, that last second, buzzer-beater wasn't luck, but a result of the hundreds of jump shots taken in practice and the time spent in the weight room – the diligent preparation you put in before the event itself.

We all know there are many ways to measure ***achievement*** and success. The important thing to remember is that you will be remembered for what you achieve and your place in history will be dependent on it. When we die, there are two dates that are printed on our tombstones – the date we are born and the date we died, separated by a dash. It is this dash that represents the life we led – including our achievements. The eulogy and program will focus on your achievements and contributions to your family and society. Everyone wants to be remembered for something positive and the more positive stories that can be retold, the stronger your legacy will be. When we talk about achievement, we really are talking about legacy – what will you be remembered for long after you are done. This is true in every field of endeavor.

This idea of achievement and legacy is most evident in the world of sports. When trying to determine who is the greatest at his respective sport, what is the first thing that the argument turns to? Rings. Championships. The discussion may start with athletic ability, but it quickly turns to who has the most Super Bowl, World Series, NBA Championship, etc. rings to his credit. The ring is the ultimate form of achievement and is tangible, so it is the go to argument when comparing athletes of different eras.

Rings are great, but you also need to focus on those areas that do not culminate in championships, but represent opportunities for achievement nonetheless. Think of the feeling you get when you do well on a test, especially a tough one. How about how you felt when you asked the pretty girl out on a date and she said yes. There may be no ring to flaunt in someone's face, but the feeling is no less exhilarating than if one was given. It is the intrinsic nature of achievement that should be your focus, not what is provided from an outside source. Things given to you by others can be taken away.

Feelings you develop from within are yours forever. The great thing about achievement is that not only is it one or several pieces of the you puzzle; it is also the culminating image. Whatever the end result it, you have made some kind of achievement, some level of accomplishment and success.

Knowledge, Awareness, Perseverance, Preparation, and Achievement. When you put these elements into play and develop them to the best of your ability, you are well on your way to assembling the puzzle that is you. It will take time for the picture to come into focus, but that is okay. All good things are difficult to achieve and take time; the bad things are easy to get. Don't rush or worry about how an event will turn out or how a piece will fit. Just know that the piece is shaped the way it is purposefully and its placement will be made evident in its proper time. As you try to figure out what your puzzle will look like, frustration will set in. When this happens, remember the words of the German philosopher Martin Heidegger: "*Anyone can achieve their fullest potential, who we are might be predetermined, but the path we follow is always of our own choosing. We should never allow our fears or the expectations of others to set the frontiers of our destiny. Your destiny can't be changed but, it can be challenged. Every man is born as many men and dies as a single one.*"

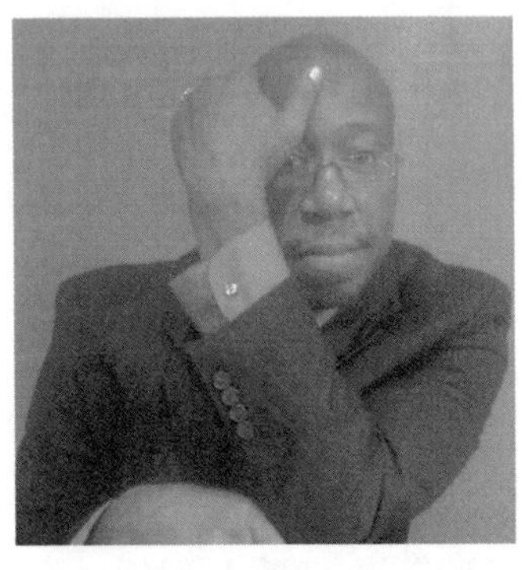

Frank Simmons, Jr. is a speaker, trainer, coach, mentor, author, and motivator. Frank has traveled extensively throughout the United States speaking to audiences of all ages and backgrounds.

He worked for Monster Worldwide as a Speaker, Trainer, Area Manager, Content Contributor, providing national speaker training and coaching and speaking to high school, college students, parents, and staff. He also spoke for organizations such as Bank of America, the Equal Employment Opportunity Council, Army ROTC, and others.

Frank is the Chief Inspirational Officer for Frankly Speaking Seminars providing workshops, seminars, coaching, training, and keynotes. Frank is the author and co-author of 4 books - The Man of Destiny, Unleash the Greatness Within You, Pursue IT with All You've Got, and My Vision, My Plan, My Now. He is also a National Trainer for Time To Teach, Moovin4ward Presentations, Rachel's Challenge, and The Art Institutes.

With over 25 years of speaking, coaching, and training experience, Frank is well equipped to help you, your company, or your organization achieve your goal of speaking publicly. He has presented to over a million people across the United States and has trained, coached, and mentored over 1000 professional speakers, coaches, singers, clergy, and business professionals.

Relationships Matter

Frank Simmons

Relationship is defined as a connection, association, or involvement between two or more persons by blood, marriage, emotional or otherwise. I want to talk to you about every relationship that I can think of. Of course, this won't be exhaustive but, I am going to do my best and hopefully you leave this chapter with some understanding.

First of all, there are some characteristics that are common to ALL relationships and they must be understood if we are going to have any success with the relationships that we have. So, if you see some common themes, don't be alarmed. The bottom line is that Relationships Matter.

There are 8 relationships that I want to discuss with you and they ALL matter. At some point in your life, you will encounter every single one of these relationships. We are going to discuss your relationship with God/Higher Power, Self, Parents/Guardians, Sibling(s), Authority/Leadership, Strangers, Friends, and lastly, The Opposite Sex. Let's get at it!

The first relationship that I want to deal with is your ***relationship with a Higher Power***. Now, some of you reading this may believe in different ways. So, let's just keep it at Higher Power. You can call it what you want to but, this relationship is the most important relationship that you will ever have. This relationship determines direction in your life and guides how you handle life and its many different variations.

My advice to you is to figure out what you believe and how you believe. We ALL believe in something or someone. So, who or what is that for you? To make this simple, I am going to give you my thoughts on someone living a traditional Christian lifestyle. You can apply this any way that is beneficial to you.

For the man that believes in this manner and lifestyle, God is his source of inspiration and power and he is the beneficiary of His love and mercy. To this man, God is more than just a name or a passing thought, God is everything.

This God is an all knowing and all powerful being that guides his every action, provides his every need, and heals his every disease. This is why this relationship is so important. But, this is not a perfect relationship because of the imperfections of man. Sometimes we get in the way and our relationship with God can suffer.

In order to make the most of your relationship with your God, your Higher Power, your Source there are some things that you can do. You have to make a commitment to making this relationship the priority in your life – first things first so to speak. If you want to strengthen this relationship, it is going to take some effort on your part. Take a look at the following list of things that you can do.

- Prayer
- Meditation
- Singing Songs
- Writing letters, poems, and Journaling
- Reading uplifting and positive books
- Listening to positive messages and music

Is this something that you have to do all day long? Not at all. Organize your day to make time for these types of things to happen. The key is this...the more time you spend doing these things and the more you incorporate them into your daily life the stronger and better your relationship will become. If you can get this relationship right, it will help you with every other relationship in your life.

The next relationship is your ***relationship with yourself***. When you look in the mirror, what do you see? Do you see someone valuable and great or do you see someone useless and no good? The way that you see yourself is the way that everyone else will see you. The way that you think about yourself is the way that others will think about you.

In order for you to have great relationships with anyone else, it is crucial that you have a great relationship with yourself. There is no way that you can truly care for or even love someone else until you can love yourself. It is more than just liking the clothes that you wear and the family that you come from. It is liking the very essence of who you are. You cannot expect anyone to want a relationship with you in any manner if you don't even want to deal with you. A relationship with myself sounds crazy but, many of your other relationships will not work if you don't get this one right.

One of our main problems is that many of us don't like to be alone. That is a problem. It is a problem because we depend on too many outside sources for validation. Validation begins with you. Approve of yourself before looking to anyone else for that. There are some very simple things that you can do to quit sabotaging your relationship with you.

- Stop the negative self-talk
- Speak positive affirmations (I am, I will, and I can)
- Take yourself to the movies and dinner
- Become physically active and improve your body image

Doing these types of things is not only beneficial to you but, they will help you in the other relationships that you will have. You cannot love anyone else, care for anyone else, or have a relationship with anyone else without doing those things for yourself.

The third type of relationship to discuss is your ***relationship with your Parents/Guardians***. The relationship between you and your parent(s) or guardian(s) is one of the most important relationships that you can have. It is from this relationship that you learn values, habits, customs, and traditions good or bad. This relationship helps to mold you into who you are because it is the first relationship that you have. For many people this was/is a good relationship. While, for many others, it was/is a bad relationship. Either way, you need to understand it.

It should be healthy, wholesome, and happy but, this relationship, like any other, becomes dysfunctional for so many people. This happens because of a lack of relationship with God/Higher Power and lack of proper relationship with self. Many lack an understanding of the roles of the parents and their role as a child. No matter how old you get, you are always the child if parents/guardians are still alive.

It is the role of the parents to provide for, care for, discipline, and instruct and it is the role of the child to respect and honor those that have been given the task of raising them. But, what about abuse? Great question. I believe that if you are in this type of situation you need to seek help immediately. That is a completely different topic and one that I don't have time to write about. If you can master being a child then you can master being a parent.

In order for this very important relationship to work everyone in the family must learn and practice their own role. This may require some work but, it is well worth it. You want to have a positive relationship with your parents/guardians.

How about your ***relationship with your siblings***? A lot of people refer to this as sibling rivalry. Why would we call it that? It shouldn't have to be labeled that way but, it is. Again, this is because we have become accustomed to fighting and arguing instead of relating. This should be one of the easiest relationships we have but oftentimes it is not.

There seems to be a struggle for the love of our parents / guardians. This need for love, acceptance, friendship, and care form our parents often turns into animosity among siblings. This should not be. You have to realize that each child is unique and requires different methods of love, acceptance, friendship, and care from their parents.

Respect your brothers and sisters and love them for who they are. You don't have to jockey for position or be someone that you are not. Your siblings should be your closest friends and biggest supporters not your rivals.

The fifth relationship to talk about is your ***relationship with authority/leadership***. Follow the leader. Get in line. Stop. Go.

Be quiet. These are commands that I have heard all of my life. These are also commands that I will hear for the rest of my life. Following is a part of life and if you cannot follow then you cannot lead. This is a principle that many people do not understand.

Somehow we believe that to follow is to be inferior. That is not the case. Following shows us how to lead. At some point, we all have to be the student. We don't start off as the teacher. Proper relationship to those in leadership expands you and makes you bigger.

Proper relationship requires respect. We can disagree and have opinions but, we must always respect those in leadership roles. The last thing that you want is to be in a rebellious relationship with authority and leadership. That causes more harm than good and it really isn't worth it.

Your ***relationship with strangers*** can have an effect on what happens to you. You have probably heard the saying, "do unto others as you would have them do unto you". You have also heard that what goes around comes around. Some people call it karma.

The dictionary defines a stranger as someone who is neither a friend nor an acquaintance, a foreigner, and a newcomer. They are people that you come into contact with at school, the mall, church, the grocery store, and many other places. How you treat and respond to them is just as important as how you treat and respond to any of your friends or family.

Have you noticed that people will walk by you and not say excuse me? Have you held the door for someone and they didn't say thank you? Have you ever seen people be treated unfairly because of color, race, religion, gender, etc.? I am sure that you have witnessed all of these things at least once in your life. Don't let the offender be you. Every person deserves kindness and respect.

As you go about your day, remember to not forget that kindness and compassion and respect can make the difference in someone else's day. When you are in right relationship with those that you don't even know, it will benefit your life greatly and in unexpected ways. You will find that those that don't know you will begin to treat you better. It is always good and right to do good and right.

The 7th relationship that I want to discuss is your ***relationship with your friends***. Friend is defined as a person attached to another by feelings of affection or personal regard; a person who gives assistance, a patron, or a supporter. We all need partnership. We all need people that care about us, assist us, and support us that are not family.

The Bible says that friends are iron sharpeners. That means that a friend is someone who has the ability to make you better. You need people around you that have different perspectives, personalities, thoughts, and ideas. These are the qualities that make it possible for you to be your best. You need friends of different races, genders, backgrounds, and religions. These are the people that enlarge your world view and help you see a whole picture not just a snapshot.

Friends will disagree with you without being angry with you and challenge your way of thinking and doing things without belittling you. It is a friction that sharpens you without breaking you. They help us gain perspective with things that are going on in our lives and help us in making decisions. But, this is not a one way street. You should be doing the same thing for them.

If you want to be a good friend, you should be the same thing to them that they are to you. You should be a good listener. You should be someone that they can confide in without judgement. They are not your child, you are not their boss, and you are not their parent. You are a friend and a friend loves at all times.

The last relationship to tackle is your ***relationship with the opposite sex***. I guess you can say that I saved the best for last. Boy meets girl. Man meets woman. Things begin to happen. Then confusion. Opposites don't want the same things or see things the same way. There are emotional and physical differences making this the most difficult relationship to master. As a matter of fact, this requires more work than any other relationship. What are you saying, Frank? I am saying that every other relationship in your life will help you be better at this relationship.

First of all, you are not ready for this kind of relationship if you don't have the right relationship with your God/Higher Power and yourself. If you have not learned how to treat others the way you want to be treated, stay away from this relationship. If you haven't learned how to respect authority and leadership, if you are still at odds with your parents and you and your siblings are still in rivalry, stay away from this relationship. If you don't know how to be a friend, you can't handle this relationship.

Let me tell you a Bible story. According to the Bible, god created Adam and gave him authority and dominion over everything that He had created. Yet, God did not create someone "for" Adam. He realized that it was not good for Adam to be alone and created Eve. This is where things get crazy.

When Adam came to, he saw this creature that God had created "for" him that was equal to him in every way with the same authority and dominion but, with a few physical differences. I could imagine him thinking, "what am I supposed to do with this"? What he was supposed to do was treat her the same way he treated God –love her with all of his heart, soul, and mind. That's exactly what he did.

When Eve decided to eat the fruit from The Tree of Life, Adam had a decision to make. Do I eat with her and risk Paradise or do I let her eat alone and lose her. He made the best choice and the only choice he could. He would rather have relationship with her outside of Paradise rather than have Paradise without her because he realized that wherever she was that's where Paradise was.

That's the kind of commitment that this relationship requires. It requires that you love this person more than you love life itself because you understand that life IS her. This relationship is not a game. It is a very serious thing.

If you want this relationship to be successful, it is going to take and unselfish approach. It takes you preferring someone else above you. That is why the relationship that you have with yourself is so important. You need to understand who you are and what makes you tick in order to have a relationship like this. You are not less than and the other person is not more than. It is a relationship with equal footing with each party practicing the things that make for great relationships – respect, care, concern, and love.

Does this mean that there will be no conflict? Not at all. Conflict and friction and disagreement and frustration are all natural occurrences in great relationships. The difference is that all of those things happen without judgement and hostility.

I hope that you can leave this chapter with a brief understanding of what relationships are comprised of. As I stated, they are difficult but necessary. Relationships enhance our lives and the experiences make us better. But, they don't just happen. They have to be cultivated and worked on. Remember this, "the quality of the relationships that we have does not depend on the length of those relationships. It depends on the intensity of the moments that we share in the building of those relationships". That's a FRANK Thought!!!

Jonathan Oliver

Jonathan Oliver is a dynamic speaker and seminar developer whose mission is to create a world of truth, love, and faith. He currently travels speaking to students of all ages about character development and leadership skills. He has been blessed with the opportunity to speak to over 3 million people.

He is the founder of Higher Enlightenment, which is a firm that provides spiritual and intelligent insight to others with the goal of helping them to believe in themselves and reach beyond their fears. He has completed his first book entitled Impersonations, co-author 3 books My Now My Vision My Plan, My Now for the Entrepreneur, My Now for the Student Leader, and is currently working on his second book where he shares how he lives and learns being dyslexic. His future endeavors include life coaching and being intimately involved in helping others fulfill their dreams.

Jonathan is an experienced speaker who has worked with companies including Toastmasters, Making it Count, Rachel's Challenge, and Moovin4Ward. He has been named a top presenter for middle school and high school assemblies. He was part of a four time division III collegiate football championship at Hardin Simmons University. He earned a Bachelor's degree in Behavioral Science with a minor in Biology. He strives to live the message that "Life is what you are born with, living is what you do with it."

Mixed Messages: Lust to Love

Jonathan Oliver

THE WOLRD'S GREATEST WANT

"The greatest want of the world is the want of godly men-men who will not be bought or sold, men who in their inmost souls are true and honest, men who do not fear to call sin by its right name, men whose conscience is as true to duty as the needle to the pole, men who will stand for the right though the heavens fall." ~ Johnny Johnson

I want the future man to be able to understand that there is more to sex then just getting girls and hooking up. I want them to understand that the idea of real love requires a way of living that is open and vulnerable. A lot of people don't talk about that right now. It's about Snap chat, Twitter, Tinder and "hooking up" websites. I want the future man to be able to read this and say, "What if I want to be in a relationship or if I wanted to date somebody? What would that look like?" These type of qualities are very attractive to the opposite person I'm trying to date versus being sneaky, reclusive, or with holding.

Let me share with you an experience I had with a young man who is 15 years old at the gym the other day. He has a girlfriend and he is a guy that looks up to me. He and his buddy hang on to every word I say. This one particular young man who is 15 years old boastfully told me he has a girlfriend with a huge smile on his face. I asked him, "What are you doing with a girlfriend? You have your whole life ahead of you to experience having a girlfriend."

He and his buddy began to look at one another shaking their heads back-and-forth while smiling and looking at me as if to say you know I why have a girlfriend. So using my right hand, I shaped my fingers as if I was pointing a gun and I placed my right hand beside my waist as if I were placing my Smith & Wesson six shooter into its holster. Then while looking into the eyes of the young man who had the girlfriend I said, "You don't pull this out or make a draw until you have this on your finger" while pointing at my wedding ring. His response and facial expression was one of bewilderment.

"Are you sure?" he asked. I continued, "You don't pull this out" looking at my imaginary Smith & Wesson six shooter, "to just play with. Things happen when you pull this out."

The young man replied that his brother and his friends told him that he needed to "pull" as many girls as he could before he got married. My rebuttal was "That is the opposite of what you need to do. You are going to have to give an account to your future wife on who you "pulled" and you are going to have to go all the way back to the beginning."

His smile now turning into a blank stare. He asked me "I can't keep that a secret?" I looked him in the eyes and said "When you go to heaven you are going to have to give an account to God for your actions. The same thing applies to your wife. You don't want to go into marriage with secrets."

To the future man my finger is now pointed at you. Those people who give you that bad advice are not going to be around when things go south. It's going be one person there to face those repercussions...you. Therein lies the problem with bad advice and bad examples.

The advice of others affects our future man. I got the same advice that young man received. Don't just date one girl. Play the field. I can recall being asked by my dad, other male relatives, and even some aunts "How many girlfriends do you have?" It was odd to me that it was not a question of having a girlfriend but of how many I had. The message I received was having anything less than one girlfriend meant something must be wrong with me. In other words, if I had only one girlfriend then I must not be doing something right. The question of how many girlfriends I had was translating to me as marker of if I was growing into a handsome, successful young man. I can see that now looking back from my mid-30s. But at that time of my life I did not have the maturity that I have now.

Here's what it lead to in my life: I saw my first pornographic image when I was around 10 years old. I started masturbating in the six grade and for the next 20 years nearly every day I either masturbated or looked at some form of porn. For some men this may be viewed as no big deal; just a rite of passage into becoming a man. But this filled me with shame, isolation, lies, obsession, and spiritual brokenness.

Then I saw first-hand pastors, deacons, and married church members who would praise God on Sunday morning but by Sunday afternoon those same people would be yelling, cussing, cheating, or shacking up. These were the people on Sunday who portrayed themselves as the model citizen or the model Christian and then the rest of the week it was a different story. Those examples made me feel that it was okay for me to be doing things I did because everyone else seemed to be living a lie. These examples helped me to justify my wrong actions.

The seeds that these experiences plant in a young man are damaging. We do not think our children are paying attention, but believe me they are. In my life I have watched the people I was supposed to emulating. I have watched my uncles, deacons, and adults in my life do and say hypocritical things. It's their actions that I saw that made such a big difference in my life. Their actions were so different from their words.

Growing up as a young boy in my world, I received many mixed messages, and more mixed messages followed. There were some good messages. I saw men provide for their household by working hard, keeping food on the table, the lights on, and clothes on the backs of their children. I heard a lot about going to school and working hard to get a good education. I was told not to have sex before marriage, not to get a girl pregnant, to wear a condom to avoid STDs, and to take care of your responsibilities if you do get a girl pregnant. But sex and sexuality, pornography, and how to have a healthy loving relationship and marriage were not spoken about unfortunately. With the lack of that guidance and clarification, those mixed messages continued to bombard my adolescent brain. I unconsciously conformed to these backward messages and replayed them in my mind where they stayed with me until I reached a place of brokenness. The messages flowed through my mind.....

1. Porn isn't that big of deal, but keep it a secret.

2. Cheating is what it is. DON'T GET CAUGHT!

3. Sex is great.

4. The more a girl does sexually the more she cares for you.

5. Masturbation is fine, but keep it a secret.

6. The stronger the orgasm, the more she really cares for you.

7. If you have great sex with someone and it's often then it must be love.

8. Work hard, go to college, and get a good education.

9. I'm going to prove to God that I'm good enough.

10. Be responsible.

Messages shape who you are and your beliefs and those were my messages.

It is easy to see that these messages do not lead to long, loving, and meaningful relationships with the opposite sex. So let us talk about some other words and messages and see how they resonate:

Transparency, authenticity, intimacy, accountability, integrity, and vulnerability are core words we should all understand. I will share three different definitions for each one of these words in order to be crystal clear with the future man and avoid any chances of mixed messages.

Transparency

-Wikipedia – one of the world's great examples of transparent collective behavior – states that "transparency" as it pertains to behavior implies openness, communication, and accountability. It is *a* metaphorical extension *of the* meaning a "transparent" object is one that can be seen through. Transparent procedures include open meetings, financial disclosure statements, freedom of information legislation, budgetary review, audits, etc.

Trust is the foundation of a relationship. Transparency is the currency of trust, the open sharing of information among parties involved.

Transparency is a way of relating to your partner in which you reveal your inner self, your true experience. That means exposing your vulnerabilities and fears, as well as your desires and points of view about whatever issues you're discussing. One is being open and revealing about yourself to your partner. It includes letting go of inhibitions or defensive feelings you might be harboring about what you haven't revealed, and also acknowledging your reluctance to do so. The flip side is being open and receptive to your partner's reality: his or her feelings, wishes, desires, fears and differences from yourself. It means openly encouraging your partner to express them to you.

Authenticity

To be authentic is to be real, transparent, truthful, or honest.

Authentic people are not afraid to be who they are and show who they are. There is no pretense. There is no building themselves up to look better; there is no tearing themselves down to look worse. They are secure with who they are. They know their strengths and use them in a loving, compassionate way. They know their weaknesses and catch themselves, without recrimination, when they fall into them. They are what we sometimes refer to as being "real." Authentic people are approachable. It doesn't matter what position they hold or what activity they are engaged in, if you are with them you will be treated with respect and attention.

Merriam-Webster defines authentic as a quality of being genuine and worthy of belief. Hence, a person who is completely trustworthy is deemed to be authentic. Yet to genuine requires a certain transparency, whereby others can witness the unfiltered personality, without any masking.

Intimacy

Intimacy is about being emotionally close to your partner, about being able to let your guard down, and let him or her know how you really feel. Intimacy is also about being able to accept and share in your partner's feelings, about being there when he/she wants to let their defenses down.

Intimacy (IN-TO-ME-YOUSEE) is all about the willingness to grant your partner total access to your inner world. Your inner world is the hidden world of your secrets, fantasies, motives, intentions, desires, and beliefs. It's who you are without the masks and without the pretenses. Achieving this state of intimacy requires you to be mentally and emotionally transparent. This is why there's no real intimacy without transparency.

Intimacy, makes us feel alive like we've been found, as if someone finally took the time to peer into the depths of our soul and really see us there. Naked and not ashamed. Respecting your partner's boundaries, respecting each other's privacy, not pressuring your partner, being faithful.

Accountability

Accountable is defined in the Webster dictionary as "Responsible; Liable". The quality or state of being accountable; an obligation or willingness to accept responsibility for one's actions.

Clear commitments that-in the eyes of others-have been kept. Accepting responsibility for self, acknowledging past use of violence, admitting when you are wrong, communicating openly and honestly, keeping your word, not making excuses for your partner's or for your own actions. Relationship is built on truth rather than game playing.

Accountability means that we have anywhere from 1 to 3 people that hold us responsible for our actions in areas of our lives in which we consistently struggle with sin, or fail to live up to God's standards. Accountability is meant to help us overcome these sinful strongholds in our lives.

Integrity

Partners are able to maintain beliefs and sense of self as well as offer time & attention to the relationship. Partners have some independence & privacy and care about each other's quality of life. Working on a relationship always begins with working on ourselves; take responsibility for our behavior (be accountable).

Integrity is not conditional and doesn't change based on the situation. It is the way you view yourself and how you conduct yourself.

Integrity means living by your code. Integrity means being undivided-a man of integrity doesn't waver between two opinions. He doesn't fold under pressure. Other men under pressure may make mistakes, but pressure only makes him more determined to do the right thing. A man of integrity stands his ground. He is not double-minded, nor easily swayed. His loyalties are not split. He cannot be corrupted. He has decided in advance to hold his position, no matter what the cost. He takes personal responsibility for his inward character and outward conduct, while trusting Christ to empower him through the Holy Spirit. Incorruptible, sound, complete. Not flawless, but determined in Christ. –Integrity excerpt from The Young Man in the Mirror by Patrick Morley

Vulnerability

Dr. Brene Brown, a distinguished author and researcher, informs us that vulnerability is often viewed as a weakness, but it's actually a strength. In her landmark book Daring Greatly, she explains that vulnerability is the core of all emotions and feelings. She writes, "To feel is to be vulnerable. To believe that vulnerability is a weakness is to believe that feeling is a weakness. To foreclose on our emotional life out of fear that the costs will be too high is to walk away from the very thing that gives purpose and meaning to living.

Vulnerability is about sharing our feelings and our experiences with people who have earned the right to hear them. Being vulnerable takes courage. But it's worth it. It's worth it to be ourselves, to connect to others.

A willingness to be vulnerable is a significant feature of lasting relationships — ones in which partners are allies, not foes.

Learning the application of transparency, authenticity, intimacy, accountability, integrity, and vulnerability in relationships and ultimately in my marriage came at a cost. For me that price of admission was pain, loss, suffering, heart-felt sorrow, brokenness, and the death of an image. The words I have just defined do not reflect or describe pornography, lust, sex, or orgasms. The messages that they send are not mixed or confusing; it's simply a message of love and acceptance.

The problem with pornography is not that it shows you so much, but that it shows you so little. Pornography implanted in my brain is an obsession of fantasy. It did not show me how to be selfless but instead it manifested more selfishness. Lust filled me with a surge of dopamine, but in the end left me feeling depleted and unfulfilled. Sex was the target, but emptiness hit the bull's-eye. Orgasms where the goal but shame, despair, and being unknown were the rewards.

The greatest gift I have is failing. It's a necessary thing. I would never let go of my deceived self because going through the brokenness and the awakening made me better. Back then if I was happy, mad, glad or sad--lust and sex were my go to drug. The thinking I had strapped to my heart and running through my brain was as follows: seeking sympathy, victim thinking, instant gratification, God doesn't want me to be miserable, blaming, uniqueness, everybody's doing it, anger, my way, the "good one", hop-over, reckless attitude, minimizing, exaggerations, manipulation, denial, misrepresenting intentions, motives, desires, and emotions. To stay in the shadows and supply the mixed messages had become my belief system.

In life, you don't rule your beliefs—your beliefs rule you and being unaware of this fact makes you dangerous. Regardless of how badly you want to live according to truth, if you have wrong thinking, then your actions will be inconsistent with your heart. A changed heart will produce a changed life. A transformed heart will produce a transformed life.

I have finally reached a place of knowing I was truly in need of a Savior and it had nothing to do with me being good enough. I had to surrender my old belief system completely. It had failed me over and over again. There is a saying "hurt people, hurt people", and I have repeatedly hurt people including myself.

God has a way of getting our attention. Lost relationships and friends were not enough to get my attention. The stronger the denial and justification, the longer the behavior persists. I had to experience the reality of knowing the brokenness from my mixed messages was leading me to wishing for death to release me from my way of living. This reality culminated to thinking death would be better than to continuing to live the way I was living, and the result of this was my marriage crumbling under the weight of my double life. I did not choose the mixed messages but it was now time for me to take full responsibility for my response, reactions, and following of those messages.

"A changed heart will produce a changed life. A transformed heart will produce a transformed life." This is what I continue to teach myself and repeat in my mind. To be known in a loving, healthy relationship, particularly a marriage, is the blessing from applying the messages and lessons of a life of transparency, authenticity, intimacy, accountability, integrity, and vulnerability. From the ashes of lust God has turned my worst into His best.

From this place of heart-felt sorrow and brokenness God displayed a new belief system in my heart…

Religion

Man reaching up to God

Man working as a means

Man keeping rules, regulations, traditions

Christianity

God reaching down to me

God paying the price for sin with salvation by grace

God releasing me from bondage and giving me freedom

My belief and view in my spirituality and faith in God is a direct relation of how I view myself and other people. My relationship with God has changed how I viewed and treated myself, which in turn has changed how I view and treat people. From lust, selfishness, and control to letting-go, trusting, and love. The consequence of me taking responsibility, surrendering, and removing my mask was my wife bestowing me with grace, mercy, and forgiveness. She did this not because I deserve it, but because of who God is.

I learned how to lead with my heart and not let my heart lead me because eventually my heart will lie to me. I learned that my bride will never be able to meet all my needs. In fact it's unfair to her and puts too much pressure on our marriage to think that she can. I learned that it's hard to remain upset, hold resentment, or be angry with my spouse while actively investing in my marriage. I learned that God purposely put me with my bride. He is allowing two sinners, flawed and broken individuals, to come together and die to one another in order to draw closer to Him; to truly become one flesh.

I learned God's love covers all sins, shortcomings, and regrets. My pride, ego, and shame will stop me from growing as a man and not strengthen my marriage if I don't surrender and trust daily. I will have to give accounts before God for my role in my marriage. I want to please Him more than I want to please my spouse. In doing so He has blessed me by drawing me closer to my bride. He has blessed me far more than I deserve. So I say to the Future Man: our habits shape who we are and our words must be consistent with our actions over the course of time. If I'm doing the right thing for the wrong reason, I'm going to end up at the wrong place. I have to have initiative and in taking that initiative I would like to share my life plan:

My Life Plan

My Spiritual Goals:

- To invite God into my heart daily. I know that apart from God I am nothing. ANYTHING that is good in me comes from God. I need to ask for God's will in my life daily, and to surrender and trust His will for my life.
- To have fun with God. To praise His name.
- To accept my weakness. What makes me closer to God is recognizing I can't do it all. I will never relapse when I'm weak, but it's me thinking I can handle it that will lead to pain and suffering.
- To love. I want to stay out of the box. No matter how hard I try my needs will never be met good enough. Love God, love others, and be authentic.

My Marital Goals:

- To remember my bride is never my problem, my bride only reveals the problem in me.
- To listen to my bride's heart more than her words.
- To enjoy my bride rather than please my bride.
- To be honest (intimate) with my bride. To be willing to hear what my bride thinks and to let her know how I feel.
- To pray with my bride and to pray for my bride. To just do life together.
- To have fun together.
- To keep the flame alive. Create times for us to have fun together.
- To support my bride's dreams and goals.
- To focus on what I appreciate about my bride rather what irritates me.
- To take care of myself so we can have more time together.

My Recovery Goals:

- To never trust me. I'll even lie to myself.
- To always be in a group of brothers who care and who really know me and are willing to share life with me. For me, this one is especially important. I'm not sure I can be totally honest, even with myself, without my band of brothers. For too often, I say, "This time I won't tell" or

"it's not that bad." But each time I meet with my guys and see them being brutally honest I know I can do it too. I can tell the truth and at that moment I'm set free. I fear what would happen if I didn't have others supporting me and whom I also support.

- To always be giving to others who need hope.
- To stop making SUBS (Seemingly Unimportant Decisions) that put me in high-risk situations.
- To be intentional when I travel or when my bride travels to keep myself safe.
- To never forget what my old nature is capable of.
- To have fun and laugh.

From the renewing of our vows to expecting our first child, it's all a miracle. There are no guarantees in the outcomes of love, marriage, or healthy relationships. However when we take care of our side of the street there is a risk in loving ourselves enough to want to live a life of transparency, authenticity, intimacy, accountability, integrity, and vulnerability. So when you make eye contact with the man reflecting back at you in the mirror the message should be clear and concise.

I encourage you to make your own Life Plan. You may not have as many goals as myself and that is acceptable. Still write down what you have. What are your spiritual, marital, and/or recovery goals?

My Life Plan

My Spiritual Goals:

1)____

2)____

3)____

4)____

My Marital Goals or Relationship Goals:

1)____

2)____

3)____

4)____

My Recovery Goals or Personal Goals:

1)____

2)____

3)____

4)____

Remember to have fun and laugh. Don't beat up on yourself but remember doing the same thing over and over again expecting different results puts you right back into insanity.

"Though no one can go back and make a brand new start, anyone can start from now and make a brand new ending."-Carl Bard

Matt Gagnon

Founder of LifeStory Coaching & Development, Matt is a Co-Active Lifestyle/Leadership Coach, speaker, author, and LinkedIn Profile Optimizer. With the belief that everyone has an EPIC life story to be told, Matt supports individuals and groups through the most challenging of chapters, helping clients find their way forward, achieve their goals, and stop playing small in life. Focusing on the power of personal branding and story, Matt helps clients articulate their values, story, and career bringing social media and resumes to life.

Matt brings over 15 years of experience with building teams, leadership development, recruiting, and developing efficiencies in both operations and customer service while working with some of the biggest brands on the planet including Staples, Cole Haan, Under Armour, Carter's/Osh Kosh B'gosh, and the San Antonio Spurs.

Matt graduated with a degree in Marketing Management from Thomas College in Waterville, Maine. In 2014 Matt attended the Coaches Training Institute to obtain his CPCC and joined the International Coaching Federation in 2015. Matt married his high school love, Nikki, in 2005. In 2013 they welcomed their son Fox Henry into the world. On Sunday's they can be found at LifeAustin Church volunteering with the children in the LifeKids program.

A Father's Legacy

Matt Gagnon

My Dad was my best friend, is not something you hear from men enough in our world today; however, Henry (Hank) Achilles Gagnon Jr. was my best friend. He was one of the funniest, coolest, frugal, loving, caring, hardworking, and intelligent dudes I have ever known. My Dad was a big guy at 6'1", heavy set frame, large bushy mustache, and wore glasses sporting a sticker on his left lens due to an injury that affected his vision. He was not only my best friend, but an amazing father, historian of music, hilarious storyteller, and a great man who was loved by many.

Here's the essence of my family dynamic. My parents divorced shortly after I was born, meaning that I would grow up with my Dad visiting me every Wednesday evening and me spending every other weekend with him. After the divorce, my mom would re-marry, and my Dad would meet the love of his life few years later. I want to make this clear from the beginning... even with the challenges of raising a family through divorce were not always easy, I was blessed to have two amazing sets of parents who did the best they knew how to do. I owe a lot of thanks and love to my step-mom who is, and always will be, a second mom to me. Our family grew a lot over the years – I have a half-sister who is two years younger through my mom, two half-sisters through my Dad who are five and ten years younger, and two step-sisters through my second step-father who are also five and ten years younger. Yes...that's FIVE sisters! I was the oldest and I was the only boy in the family. No pressure on me, but I was last hope of continuing the Gagnon family name. That hope turned into a reality by 2013 when my wife and I welcomed a beautiful little boy into the world – Fox Henry Gagnon. Cool name...right?! His middle name would be after my Dad and my Grandfather. The origin of his first name came to me in a dream several years ago – I dreamed that someday I would have a son named Fox. That dream came true; however, it took several years to talk my wife into naming our son Fox...which she finally agreed to the day he was born. Actually, she wanted to name him Jackson...which is a strong name, but it just didn't feel like the right name for our son. On the day he was born, the nurse walked into the room and asked us what name we chose for our new baby boy. When we said Fox, she said with great excitement, "what a cool name, and finally not another Jackson"! Apparently there had been a flurry of Jackson's born within the past several weeks. I digress...but for the record, my son was born just weeks before the "What Does the Fox Say?" song became an international sensation! My wife is amazing in supporting my relentless passions in life.

Throughout this chapter I will share the key values of fatherhood from my perspective as a son and as a father today. My goal for all men, regardless of what your experience was like with your Dad, is to show how a father can create an incredible legacy, even in the most challenging of situations.

Being Present

There are two major dates in my life that will forever be engraved in my heart – April 29, 2013 and June 6, 2013. They evoke a powerful and eclectic array of emotions. From that I learned many lessons about being present and how to honor my values.

In many different ways, I witnessed my Dad being present throughout my. I can't imagine what it would be like as a father who can only see his son a few days a month; however, that was his reality. When my mom re-remarried, we moved about ninety-minutes away from where my Dad lived in Waterville, ME. We ventured deep into the isolated woods of Phillips, ME. No joke...it was a very remote village with a population that was less than a thousand people. I am fairly certain that the moose-to- people ratio was 2:1; however, I zero data to support that statement. My Mom and Dad remained friends over the years and my Dad would take a job working as a maintenance man for the Housing Authority in Waterville – the same company that his ex-mother-in-law was the director (my grandmother). My Dad would drive about ninety-minutes one way every Wednesday (sometimes longer due to weather) to visit me for a couple hours and then make the long drive back. He would repeat the same trip every other weekend to pick me up so I could spend weekends with him in Waterville. Not once did I ever hear him complain.

As a child I wasn't aware of what it must have been like for my Dad to do all of the super awesome Dad stuff he did for me. He was a full-time father in his heart but physically only able to be with me part-time. By my junior year of high school, it clicked. I finally had my driver's license and I started to make the drive to spend every-other weekend with him. It was during those drives that I started to reflect on what my Dad's emotional journey must have been like all those years and how much I appreciated him for being there as much as he could be.

In 2006 my wife and I relocated to Austin, TX. It was difficult to leave my family behind, but it was for an incredible career opportunity. I also knew that if I had to experience one more Maine winter, I was going to lose my mind. Even with 2,200 miles between us, my Dad and I would still talk at least three times a week on the phone and he would come to visit two or more times a year. By April of 2011, I was going through a very challenging and low period in my life. I remember calling my Dad..."Hey Pop, I really need you here...going through a lot of stuff". He told me it wasn't really possible to come down at that moment but maybe in another month. My Dad wasn't a spontaneous person...he was a planner and he liked cheap plane tickets, so flying at the last second was an expensive idea; however, five minutes after that call, he called back and said he was flying out in a couple days to spend a week with me. That was superhero stuff to me, and I was a grown man at the time. My Dad tended to think with his wallet first but his heart always made the right choice. Honestly, I wish I was as responsible with money as he was.

Being present with your kids (or spouse, friends, etc.) is not just about being physically there. Present means being engaged with those around you. This means your children get all of your attention where you are listening and interacting with them. This level of engagement allows you as a father to hear and feel the things that are not being said. My Dad didn't just hear that I wanted him to come see me in Texas; he heard and felt the urgency in my voice.

- Be engaged with your children – interact, listen, and play.
- Listen to what is not being said – your kids are saying so much more than what is being spoken. Get connected and deepen your learning of what's really happening.
- Trust your intuition – It's never wrong.

- Know that your kids are always watching and learning from you – even the smallest moments can create long lasting memories.

Laughter

Laughing with my Dad...they are some of my favorite memories. I often shared those moments with my two sisters through my Dad and Step-mom. He was a hilarious guy! When we were not laughing at something he was saying or doing, we were laughing about something he had done or said. A great example is when he was complaining about gas prices while we were running errands in town. After his long rant, I sarcastically replied "Great job finding the silver lining"! Without skipping a beat, he leaned his head out of my jeep window, looking up to the sky with a childlike wonder, and said "Where is it". He was genuinely looking to the sky for a silver lining! I was so lucky to have my sisters present to witness that conversation.

My Dad lived life with a unique, and somewhat unscrewed, perspective. What do I mean by an "unscrewed" perspective? One of the best examples is from his own Facebook page where he posted: "Hank Gagnon discovered he can throw a leaf blower at least seventy-feet as the seven devils of Buddha were escaping his blown mind. It just didn't want to start". His speech often flowed in an oddly poetic manner, with a Christopher Walken like flair, sputtering out an eclectic vocabulary of real and mostly made-up words. For the record, Dad was a huge Christopher Walken fan. He insisted on doing impressions of him at every family gathering...it was an awful impression but I think that's what made it so funny. He described himself as a noted raconteur, drummer, bon vivant, and a beer specialist – claiming that he graduated from Oxford as a Rhodes Scholar with a degree in Quarks and String Theory. I remember him giggling like a little girl the day he posted it online. He claimed to have invented the word "onamonapia". Actually he didn't know the meaning of the word or that it already existed! He truly believed that he just made it up. He had unique names for my sister's and me: Mr. Festoon, Feziwig, Fez, Chicken, the Ole Chicken, Tahtaah bird, Teetee bird, and many more that I don't even know how to spell. The family dogs were not safe either. In fact, they had the most unusual names: festering sandwich bag, lice-E-animal, flee ridden savage, plastic pig (which was also used to describe political figures he disagreed with, along with anyone who worked in Time Warner customer service).

What I learned from him about laughter was how it could bring people together, how it could defuse conflict, how good it was for the soul, how it made life a lot less serious, and how it offered a different perspective when thinking from a place of humor and being light hearted. I also learned how laughter can also drive people away when we are reckless with how we use our words and the audience we are sharing with. Now while my Dad had a heart that was larger than life, there were a few times that his humor was not well received, and it created some awkward moments. In the Gagnon family we referred to these slips of the tongue as having a genetic disorder called Full Blown Ass Syndrome – FBAS. Please note that FBAS is not a real disorder; however, it is very real in my family...we still fight for a cure. What I loved about my father in those awkward moments was his ability to be humble, admit his mistake, and try to make it right...unless you worked in customer service at Time Warner Cable...in those situations, you were always wrong.

- Laugh with your children – they will remember those moments more than any other. They are the memories that will bring everlasting joy to the heart.
- Appreciate and encourage the unique sense of humor that your children have – it will teach them to appreciate who they are and that's all they need to be.
- Teach your children that while words are funny, how we use them can also cause hurt – know your audience and always come from a place of respect and love. If you forget to think before you speak, be humble enough to apologize and learn from it.

Share Your Gifts, Values, and Beliefs

As men and as fathers, we all have unique talents, gifts, and skills. Showing up in life with those gifts will leave a lasting impact on your kids as they discover and grow into their unique selves.

I learned the art of negotiation at a young age when we started collecting baseball cards together. He taught me how to take care of them and how to look up the value for each one. We would go to all the card shows in town, and at ten-years-old, I would buy, sell, and trade my cards with other dealers who were four times my age. It was a lot of fun and a skill that I have developed and has served me well over the years. Dad taught me that if I could find my leverage in a trade or sale, that I would have the winning advantage. Sometimes his lessons on collecting valuables were a bit intense. Every odd little trinket looked like a potential treasure. Do you know how hard it is not to read your comic books at the age of ten because you might ruin the condition or choosing not to play with your new action figure because it will decrease its value?

My Dad loved music. He was a walking vault of rock 'n' roll knowledge that was undefeatable in any trivia faceoff. He shared his love for music with me at an early age. For my seventh birthday he bought me an assortment of cassette tapes with a bright red canvas storage case that zipped shut and had a black carrying strap. It was loaded with all types of rock genres. He wanted me to discover music on my own. He didn't push any type of music on me but encouraged me to be open minded (except for country music...he didn't care for it). I settled on rock music from 1965-1975. This was also within his wheelhouse. There was something about the music during that decade that was pure magic to me. I could hear the stories they were telling through the lyrics and feel the expressed emotions coursing through my soul. We even had the same favorite song and didn't realize it until the day I heard it playing and declared that it was my favorite song of all time. It was The Who song "Baba O'Reily" from their "Who's Next" album. After telling my Dad how much I loved that song, he leaned in and pointed to his chest with a slight grin saying "it was my favorite first". It was a funny and very genuine moment that I cherish to this day. My love for music transitioned into a love for vinyl records. We would hit up all the record stores and search for the rarest and most unique albums out there. He had all the musical knowledge, and I had all the knowledge on what made one version of an album rarer than the other. We had countless conversations about music. He would always challenge me to listen to more obscure hits. In fact, he would scour YouTube every night, searching for rare gems to share with his audience. One of the best compliments he gave me as an adult was when he was putting together his dream team of people for a music trivia contest. He rattled off a few close friends and then said "probably have Matt on the team as my dark horse". This was high praise my friends! It was a sign of respect, and I lit up inside, that he not only picked me to be on his fictional team, but that he recognized and valued my knowledge.

Now listening to music and playing music was a totally different experience. My Dad played drums and supported me as a kid playing the alto saxophone – which I still play to this day. I progressed to the acoustic guitar and also found a true love for singing. My Dad was a great drummer but he held it as something very private. It was his time where he would zone out and just let the beats flow. I felt the same way about singing. It was something that I did privately for a long time. Singing in front of others was the most naked feeling I could experience. It was like giving people a window into my soul. For me, listening to music became my way of experiencing my emotions, while playing music became my way of expressing emotions. There is one short video clip of my Dad playing drums in a band during a local Blues Festival. It was one of the first times I remember my Dad saying he was nervous about playing drums; however, once he stepped into the moment, he had found his bliss. I long to have this love of music passed on to my son someday. All of the albums that I own today will someday be his, including the albums that used to belong to my Dad.

I know my Dad had a relationship with God. He casually talked about it with me from time to time and we also casually attended Catholic Church. Those moments didn't define his faith in my eyes...It was in his actions where I really saw his faith. One memorable example was when he came to visit me in Austin, TX. I watched him interact with a homeless man outside the store we were all shopping in. After a long exchange, I saw my Dad hand the man some money along with a handshake. My Dad said the guy had a long story about getting a new job and needed some extra cash. My Dad felt like he was probably being scammed, but he gave the homeless man some money anyways. I asked him why he gave him the money if he felt he wasn't being honest. My Dad looked me in the eyes and simply replied "you never know if it's God you're talking to". There was tenderness in his voice. He said it from his heart. It may seem like a small insignificant moment to some; however, it was a powerful and defining moment for me.

My Dad had a lot of unique gifts and skills. What I learned from him was that our gifts have value, and they are not always financial. Leveraging our gifts can serve, not only ourselves, but others as well. I learned this with singing. When I finally had the courage to share it with others, I saw how my vulnerability connected me to everyone else in the room.

- Recognize your unique gifts and talents – share them with your children and help them discover their own.
- Encourage your children to show up in life and teach them how their gifts will not only serve themselves but

those around them – ensure that you are doing the same by showing up in your own life.

- Know that by helping your kids discover their gifts in life, you are also teaching them about healthy expression of their feelings – a lesson that will serve them for a lifetime.
- Be the spiritual leader of your family – it's the most important role you have.

Passing of the Torch

April 29, 2013 – My son, Fox Henry Gagnon, was born. It was a long birth process but both my son and my wife came out of it healthy. It was the happiest moment of my life. I remember when I first saw my little boy, I felt like I was born to be a father. It was as if I had waited my entire life just to meet him. In that moment I remembered one thing from our birthing class, and that was how important skin to skin contact is for newborns...so I removed my shirt and held him against my skin so he would feel safe and loved...unconditionally loved. My Dad and family entered the room shortly after and we all shared the moment. My favorite memory from that day is sitting with my Dad on the couch in the hospital room. He is holding his grandson and has his arm around me. He didn't have to say a word...I could feel his love for me and for his grandson. My family flew back to Maine a couple days later.

Before he left, he put his hands on my shoulders, and with tears in his eyes, told me that I would be a great Dad, and he pulled me in for a huge hug. My heart was overflowing…

June 6, 2013 – My Dad passed away from a heart-attack early in the morning. The night before we talked on the phone like we always did, not knowing it would be the last time I would ever hear his voice. Before we hung up the phone, we both said I love you one more time. The next morning I received the phone call from my step-mom…"your Dad's not breathing" she cried. He was not feeling well that morning and decided to lie down for a bit. Within minutes of lying down he stopped breathing. The EMS team worked hard trying to revive him…but he was gone. I remember when my Dad lost his father…it was one of the first times I saw my Dad cry. I lost my best friend…I wasn't ready to lose him. I cried like I have never cried before…I begged God to save him…my heart was shattered.

My wife was already in Maine for her grandmother's funeral and I was in Texas with my month old son while my mom was in town visiting for the week. She was a superhero in that moment and I am so thankful she was with me. She gave me some cash out of a paper envelope and told me to get home that night. She wasn't going fly out for another two days but she stepped up and did some amazing "Mom Stuff". She offered to take my infant son, along with all of his stuff and would fly back to Maine. So I booked a flight for that night…It was the longest trip home of my entire life. I remember breaking out into tears throughout the entire trip. Once there, it was comforting and conflicting being in the old house with my step-mom and two sisters but no Dad. My step-mom is one of the most courageous people I know...Within the past few years she managed to beat the living shit out of breast cancer while losing her sister unexpectedly, and then the man she loved for almost 30 years...and yet she was still standing tall when I saw her; however, she wanted my wife and I to sleep in the master bedroom so we would have a quiet space for my son once he arrived with my mom in a couple days. That night I slept on his side of the bed...his things were still on the nightstand and floor. It was difficult to deal with; however, I was so exhausted from crying and traveling that I passed out pretty quickly. The next morning I remember cleaning up the iodine stains on the carpet from where the EMS team had worked on him. It was an unspeakable feeling of how much I was in shock of him leaving this world. The most difficult task was not the funeral, but packing up his drum kit. My step-mom, with a full heart, asked me if I would pack up his drums downstairs...I didn't expect it to be such a hard task; however, dismantling his drum kit brought me to tears. I remember my hands shook as I unscrewed each drum, each symbol, and stacked them up along the wall. It broke my heart into even smaller pieces, because it was another reminder that he was gone.

When I look back, I see how blessed I was to have him as a father. At the funeral I decided I would speak. The church was packed...I mean jam packed with friends and family. I was told by many that speaking would be really hard to do and it would be ok if I chose not too; however, I felt compelled to honor my father's legacy. I stood in front everyone with my two sisters behind me and began to speak from my heart. I was also strengthened by my month-old son who was sitting quietly in the front row of the church. My son unknowingly provided so much healing for my family during this time of loss. As I spoke from my heart I noticed my words were not about regret. My words were about how nothing was left unsaid when he passed. I had thanked him for all the lessons he taught me in life, we respected and loved each other, and he was with me for the birth of my son. Not everyone can say that their Dad was their best friend...but I can, and for that reason, I am very blessed. What was very special about the funeral was at the end...the family all agreed that we would have a soundtrack for Dad as he was carried out of the church. I selected the last three tracks of the Beatles album, Abbey Road: Golden Slumbers, Carry That Weight, and The End. The songs symbolized the end of the Beatles. I have a quote from Golden Slumbers above my son's bed..."Golden slumbers fill your eyes. Smiles awake you when you rise. Sleep little darling, do not cry, and I will sing you a lullaby". To this day, I still feel the tears well up in my eyes every time I hear that song;

however, my tears today are also because I miss him with all my heart.

Today I am proudly living that title of "World's Best Dad" on my coffee mug. I look forward to our adventures together in life. He lights up my heart every day and I would do anything for him. He was my inspiration to find my bliss. I wanted to teach my son early on that it is never too late to write your own comeback in life and pursue your passion. Shortly after the funeral, I started my own traditions: I play vinyl records for him every month, I play guitar and sing for him, I laugh with him, and I pray with him. I will teach my son that his ability to be vulnerable will be his greatest strength. He will learn that his strength is determined by his character and not just by his physical capabilities. I will continue to lead by example and be present with my son; because I know that every day is a gift.

I love you Dad...I miss you every day. I honor your legacy by passing on the lessons you taught me to my son. I hope that this chapter not only serves the men who experienced similar stories with their father's but also to the men who had challenging relationships with their father's and are now longing to learn how to break the cycle.

Rodney Burris

Educator, National Speaker, Youth and Family Advocate, and Entrepreneur; these are some of the words used to describe Rodney Burris. In addition to a wide range of career experience, the common thread among all his ventures is a strong desire to strengthen communities.

Mr. Burris holds a BA in Psychology from the Johns Hopkins University and an MS in Management of Nonprofit Agencies from Capella University. He is deeply rooted in neighborhood empowerment and has tutored struggling students, encouraged area leaders to become more involved in the community, and reconnected fathers with their children, advising them on parenting and life skills.

Rodney is also an avid promoter of business development and entrepreneurship. His combined knowledge of non-profit experience and business-startup has been used to assist scores of interested learners. He is also one of the featured authors of the book, My Vision, My Plan, My NOW!

RodneyBurris@mail.com
www.RodneyBurris.com
@RodneyCBurris

Fat Ladies Sing All the Time

Rodney Burris

The one piece of advice I wish I would have had was about marriage.

Sometimes you are head over heels in love with her, and other times you can't stand to be around her.

And guess what, it's all normal.

Being married, your connection with her will go through natural cycles. These cycles are common and recurring. Sometimes, at the bleakest stages of our relationship, when everything is dark and midnight seems to be perpetual, we are taught to believe it's over; the proverbial fat lady has sung, and we need to pack it up, and move on with our lives. That may be true for some of us. But for most of us, the reality is, it always gets darkest before the dawn, the sun will rise again on our situation, and all of it (the fights, the bumps, the growing apart at times), is all natural. It's a natural cycle and it has happened, and will continue happening, throughout the course of life--in everybody's life--as long as we remain on this great green earth.

In fact, everything in life goes through these natural cycles.

For example, nature's building block is the atom, and it is no exception to this rule. Atoms have electrons that spin around a nucleus in a cyclical orbit. During this cycle, the atom is more prone to bond with some elements than others, its magnetism slightly changes and then reverts back, and the weight of the atom gets dispersed gyroscopically all on a microscopically small level.

One of nature's largest objects, our dear old planet Earth, also follows suit with this idea. The planet goes through seasonal cycles of winter, spring, summer and fall. As it does, life on the planet dies, regenerates, stabilizes, and breaks down at various points through each of the seasons along this cycle. Just as the planet nears the end of one of these phases along its cycle a new one kicks in, and this happens repetitively, over and over again, almost without end.

We can also find examples of this life cycle in other areas of life. Let's start with some of the smallest creatures: single-celled organisms. These are eaten by tiny sea creatures, which are eaten by fish, which are eaten by larger ocean-dwelling mammals, which are hunted by humans, which eventually pass away. What happens to their degrading bodies? Well they are broken down by the very same single-celled creatures that started this whole process. This is the food chain, which is also known as the circle (cycle) of life.

The circle of life is everywhere. Our relationships are no exception.

While connected to her, your relationship will go through very natural seasons of summer, winter, spring, and fall. Unlike the seasons that happen out in nature, these don't have predictable time lengths, and pre-calculable start/end dates. But without fail, however, these seasons will almost always loop background. Our problem? We tend to view all "Falls (autumns)" as the "beginning of the end"; the mini-deaths of winter we almost always view as "the finality", and thus our signal to get out; the newness of spring as true love; and the blinding heat of summer as unfailing passion. However, because nature teaches us that more than likely these phases are both temporary and recurring, it is to our benefit to get good at identifying them when they happen, as well as predicting their course of action as they play out (similar to a weatherman's forecast).

It is in this way, we learn to not look at every bad time in our life with her as the reason to exit. Likewise, we don't foolishly allow ourselves to believe that every blazing romance will last in its intensity, forever. Let's take a closer look at the parallels between our relationships and the natural, seasonal life cycles.

In the SPRING of your relationship, everything is new. You buzz with the expectancy of being around her, talking to her, seeing her, and spending time with her. Everything is fresh, including the physical intimacy. Oh of course, to be fair, she has some aspects that are a little annoying, but those minor chills we brush aside like pollen in the breeze; we sneeze and get over it. This is new, this is life, this is Living; and it feels good. -- We are in a Spring...

Soon after that, you reach SUMMERTIME; your relationship becomes bound, bright and balanced, like solid gold. You and her together are a well-oiled machine. Fueled by the strength and stability of your union, you guys progress along like two equally-minded partners, mutually clear on the decided task and comfortable in your respective role(s). Secure in this season, and restfully believing that all it takes is but a little maintenance to maintain this state, you often wonder how/why other couples don't have what you two have, and why they often make 'being-together' so hard. You find yourself making statements like, "Our sex life is good; if we aren't intimate ___ number of times in a week/month/day, we'll know something is wrong"; fully expecting that situation to never become a reality. You also find yourself making statements about your communication style, noting how easy you two can connect and relate. You don't mean to point out the faults of others' relationships; yours is just a heartfelt, honest recognition that if couples took the time to go on that stroll together, sit in front of that fireplace, take that shared shower, etc, then they too would have what you two are so freely accessing. At this stage of your life, you know that communication is the basis of all relationships, and you recognize that you two have hit on a surefire way to make communication work for you two. It's a great feeling. Going down the list, the same can be said for the other major aspects of a relationship. Money, for example although not as fluid and abundant as you may like, is not a source of major contention for you two. That's because you two have concluded that the amount you make together, regardless of who makes what, 'works for us', and with this you are both comfortable. The same can be said for the other factors that tend to be major issues in relationships: extended family, friends, work-life-recreation balance, etc. In all of these areas, you guys are simply 'good'; together, you two are strong and you know it. You have found the formula, and know how to make it work. In fact, it's hard to see any possible means of an 'end' in sight. *"Why break up, when we can just do these _____ things in order to re-strengthen our bond and make it grow."* In fact, couples that break up all around you are an anomaly to you, and are the epitome of why people don't apply good common practices in their relationships. -- By all means, enjoy this bliss, this bond. You are basking in the Summer sunshine of your relationship, and it feels good. There is a lot value here, a lot you can take with you into the rest of the seasons. So enjoy it!

Like any summer sun, after a while things will naturally start to cool off in your relationship, and AUTUMN begins to approach. Let's be clear, this isn't the "end" or anything. It's just that you find yourselves being less intimate (physically), and guess what, it's okay. It's actually very comfortable. Also, you two may not spend as many hours talking face to face, but again, that's also okay, because you both feel like you have a pretty firm understanding of what each other wants, what each other needs, and what the other may be thinking in any given moment, about any common circumstance. You know what makes her tick, and you feel like, for the most part, she understands you. Even when she gets angry, it's predictable. "I knew she was gonna get like that, as soon as I saw/said/heard....". Sometimes, you find yourself repeating little squabbles with each other, and yes those are annoying, but they are not the 'end of the world', and you can function just fine right through them. You two are just...comfortable. It's not highly passionate, but it's nowhere near horrible. And yes, it is routine, but it doesn't quite feel 'stale'. It's just, *'what we do'* and *'who we are'*. And to be honest, a part of you kind of relishes in the lessened time it takes to satisfy her needs; you enjoy spending less time hearing the hours about her day/friends/coworkers/experiences, because you really just want to relax in the comfort of your own home. Quickies are nice, but all the energy it takes for a full-out love-making session...the thought of that alone is draining...so, you kind of welcome the reduced frequency of physical relation. All in all, the experience is just becoming regular, relaxed, and routine; familiar, like an old glove, comfortable, like room temperature water. It's Autumn in your household, and frankly, you're okay with that.

There is a reason why we refer to "the 'dead' of WINTER" when talking about this next season. Life is dead. Growth has stopped, and the Love is gone. She no longer wants you to be close to her physically, and freezes up at your touch (...we call this 'frigid'). The warmth of a loving household is all but a memory, and you *wonder why you even ever got yourself involved in this situation in the first place* (especially given all the 'warning signs' that we are convinced have always been there, but we simply chose to ignore). Everything seems dead. Everything feels hopeless, with little to no chance of survival, and the thought of reviving the situation seems like a longshot at best. Even familiar landmarks outside seem dismal and dim; the tree that you two had your first kiss under, looks skinny, decayed and forgotten. The pool that you two used to use for romantic getaways is closed, covered-up and too cold for comfort. Even venturing over to do vital things like go to school, go to work, go visit friends or family, is a tremendous undertaking, characterized by an extreme amount of covering up and bundling up just to make it from one point to the next. The effort involved is almost discouraging of any potential reward that the destination may bring. Waking up in the morning, the house feels cold; the same lingering, nagging cold that bugged you all the way to bed the night before, has hovered around, and is the first presence that greets you when your eyes open. -- It's interesting that we used the word 'presence', because the cold in our house almost feels like another presence, another being, another entity, driving us apart, keeping us from re-connecting. Yet, oddly enough, somehow this cold presence feels...natural...as if it belongs there. When we talk about the cold in our house, we somehow make perfect sense on what it is doing there and why it should stay. In some weird sense of comfort, the cold seems to protect us from further potential hurt from our partner, and somehow, we don't really want it to go away. We don't like to be cold, but it has been cold for so long, that we've simply learned how to adjust. We can't imagine our lives without coats, scarves, hats, gloves (i.e., things that protect us from the cold), so these things have somehow become second-nature to us. But consciously, we are aware that we are cold, we are sick of it, and we want the cold (and the source of the cold) to just go away, so that we can go back to living life more comfortably. We feel like the situation will never end, that it has been like this for far too long as it is, and we would be more comfortable if we made our escape to warmer, greener pastures. We are in a Winter... and it Sucks.

Just like in nature, these are the seasons that we all will experience in our relationships. It is normal, it is natural, and each one will come, go, and repeat, in its own turn.

Our problem is often that we are not taught to expect these seasons to come. Instead, we are taught to believe that each season is an instance of eternity. We get married in the Spring because we feel that it will 'always be' this new, so we pounce on it. We don't take the time to expose ourselves to the other weather conditions we will experience with this person, thus, we have no idea if our individual ways of coping are mutually compatible together. When we hit the Summer, we believe the bliss is sustainable, when instead the highs of this season must give way to the harvest of the next season and its cooler temperatures. Looking up one day, we find ourselves in the dull drones of Fall-living, and simply resign ourselves to a life of complacency. Because nothing on our earth changes without discomfort (...for even as the saying goes, 'necessity', is the true mother of invention...), the Winter comes as growth point, to urge us into discomfort, so that we can make the changes we need to go into the new year. Instead, however, we look at it as the beginning of the end, a non-changing, bitterly cold reality that we must end (How fortunate would we be, if we were taught to view this time as a winter wonderland, enjoying the skiing and the snow and the warmth of closeness, family and giving...).

That's for some of us. Others of us are taught to expect the seasons, but not in a cyclical nature. Instead, we look at them as progressions towards an end point. Again, like before, we are taught to marry in the spring, work towards the summer, that it will eventually devolve into a boring, miserable Fall, and that we are to get rid of it in the winter. We are taught that the winter season in our relationship means that it is over, and we are not taught to expect the season to change again (although we see it happening year of year, all around us, in life).

The truth is, more than likely, these seasons will repeat in our life. These seasons are real. They will happen, and it's best to prepare/dress accordingly for each season in its due time.

HOWEVER, there is one more component to this whole equation; unlike in nature, these seasons in our relationship don't necessarily have to follow each other in the same succession each time. A boring Fall could give way to a rejuvenated Spring, without ever really hitting the icy chills of a cold winter. Likewise, one false emotion, one misunderstood/ miscommunicated comment could throw the shine of the Summer sun into the dead of the winter almost in a flash. Even the newness of the relationship as we find in Spring could very easily subside into the doldrums of Autumn by two people who don't believe that they deserve or want more/better in life; this same jump from spring to fall could happen to two individuals who are simply too busy to shoot for the stars, and prefer (either consciously or subconsciously) the predictability of a relationship in its Autumn.

And so many more permutations could happen. Just look at Mother Earth for examples: there are some regions that only have a sauna-Summer session that causes dearth, and then extremely rainy sessions that cause flood. There are some areas that never come out of the cold, and so their Springs are brisk and crispy and their Summer times are non-existent. There are some regions that experience sunshine for six months of the year, followed by six months of darkness. And the list could go on; mountainous, desert regions, open tundra, rainforests, etc.

Regardless of what variation you find in your relationship, there is a natural parallel to it. Understanding your climate and phases within the cycle with whom you are choosing to marry is absolutely paramount for sustained success. Almanacs provide clues on the general climate and weather a particular area could experience. Likewise, developing a sort of reference for yourself, will help you when times get hard, and will provide a source of healthy mental balance when times are blissfully great. -- This is not to say that your relationship should never come to an end (on the contrary, nature itself teaches us about life, death and transition). Instead, this writing is to serve to level-set our expectations of the natural phases within the life cycle that simply signify season as opposed to termination.

Knowing the seasons of your relationship cycle is wisdom; being aware of this wisdom as you navigate through them provides one with understanding. So, regardless of what it looks like, and even if all the signs are pointing towards the end, don't give up hope just yet.

Let the proverbial fat lady sing. It doesn't mean your marriage is over.

Michael L. Daniels

Michael L. Daniels is the founder and Chief Executive Officer of two entrepreneurial ventures, Incisive Technology Incorporated and Scripture Coins, LLC.

Over the past two decades, he has demonstrated his ability to build solutions for clients using knowledge and experience that effectively blends information technology, business management and a common sense approach to consulting.

One of his core beliefs is that education – whether formal or informal – is the key to success in life's ventures. His educational pursuits include studying law at Georgetown University Law Center, business management at New York Institute of Technology, and computer science at Alabama A&M University.

He is passionate about helping others reach their goals. Whether it is through software products, mentoring, counseling, or training, he finds his greatest joy in and measures his success by the level of success that he helps others attain.

He is married to Mrs. Jerylen Lavender Daniels. They have three wonderful children and have been married for nearly 20 years.

www.incisiveinc.com
www.scripturecoins.com

Problems, Opportunities, Solutions & Success

Michael L. Daniels

Too many people see a problem as a bad thing. It really doesn't matter what you call it – common terms include problem, challenge, crisis, and difficulty... it's is all a matter of perspective. People, who have a mind for success, focus on the solutions and the opportunities while the rest of the world focuses on the problems. Look at it this way, when the world was covered in darkness after sunset and the only available light came from candles, lanterns and other flames, Thomas Edison didn't focus on things like the dangers of open flames or the cost of oil for lanterns. He focused on creating the light bulb. In the same regard, Garrett A. Morgan didn't focus on traffic accidents at intersections; he focused on creating a traffic signal. Countless inventions were brought to bear because someone took the time to see past the problem and focus on the opportunity for success that comes with finding a solution. If your goal is to be successful, the first step is to train yourself to look for solutions while the rest of the world complains about the problem. However, simply finding the solution is not enough, you have to take the additional step of actually implementing the solution. Remember success begins with thought, but is consummated in action.

Step 1: Fear Not!

It's normal to be a bit nervous when faced with a problem. In reality, you may be downright scared. Indeed, fear is the first enemy that you must conquer in the battle for success. Fear has a way of keeping your mind focused on the problem and all of the bad things that can happen. Fear has the tendency to paralyze everything from your mind to your body. Fear is an unfortunate reality. Fortunately, the way that you respond to fear is up to you. That's right, *you* choose how much power fear has over you. When it comes to life's problems, you defeat fear by focusing on the solutions. You defeat fear by being bold enough to act on the solution. You defeat fear by taking action while fear tries its best to stand in your way.

Make no mistake. Fear has its proper place. It's appropriate to listen to fear in situations that could affect your overall safety and wellbeing. Let's take an example. Imagine that you are at the top of the Empire State Building, you look down and see the streets hundreds of feet below you and, suddenly, your only desire is to get down to ground level. Fear is appropriate if it keeps you from jumping off of the building. However, if that same fear makes you hold onto a rail or bench for dear life, fear is winning the battle. In this case, success is defined as getting to ground level safely. How do you move beyond fear and accomplish your goal? Simple, you let go of the rail and take the elevator to the ground floor. If the elevator isn't available you take the stairs! Defeating fear isn't about being reckless or taking unnecessary risk. It's about finding ways to reach the goal and taking action in spite of the fear.

Step 2: Weigh your Options.

When facing a problem, consider the possible outcomes. What is the worst that can happen? What is the best possible outcome? Think about what you can do to bring about the best results. Now weigh the cost. Sometimes success is found in solving a problem. Sometimes, it is found in walking away. How do you know the difference? Weigh the cost against the benefits. There are some things that you should never consider giving up to reach a goal – for example, your integrity, your faith, your family and your values. These are things that cannot be replaced and they are the things that very few people recognize as true wealth. It has been said that there is no profit in gaining the whole world if you lose your soul in the process. Many people have given up their greatest blessings in pursuit of success only to find out that they reached their goal but had lost more than they gained. Right now – in this very moment – you have the opportunity to make some decision about how you will act if faced with certain situations. That's right, you can decide now, among other things, that you will never lie, cheat or steal. And, when faced with the opportunity to do such things, your actions will be pre-determined and you won't have to struggle with the choice in the heat of the moment. If the cost isn't something irreplaceable, consider which is more important, the goal or what it will cost you to achieve it. Look at from every angle. What will it cost in terms of money, energy, and time? Look beyond the immediate benefits and consider how this decision will affect your life in three months, three years and even three decades. Once that's done, choose wisely and move forward.

Step 3: Move Forward!

Now that you have conquered fear and weighed the options, the only thing left to do is move forward. Set your eyes on the goal, and press for the mark. Don't allow yourself to be distracted or discouraged. Take on the virtues of patience and persistence. Patience will help you avoid the need for instant gratification while persistence will help you to stay the course. You will surely run into obstacles on your path to success, but don't give up. Find your way over, under, around or through the obstacles and once you have passed them, don't look back. When you encounter a new obstacle, remember your victories over the obstacles of the past and know that you can keep moving forward. Do a little bit every day. Make steady progress – step-by-step and day-by-day. It doesn't matter whether your step covers an inch or a yard. What is important is that you continue taking the steps until you reach your goal. Keep going, your future is what you make it. Start making it today!

Lonnie Mathews

Lonnie Mathews is a motivational financial speaker who empowers audiences with tools and strategies to make immediate and long-term shifts in their lives. Lonnie has worked as a financial advisor and is the author two books on personal finance. His latest title *Spend Everything – an inspirational guide to money management* is available where books are sold. Lonnie now travels the country delivering his powerful and life changing messages on personal finance. Lonnie is a dynamic and engaging speaker who gets audiences excited about taking charge of their financial futures.

Lonnie@lonniemathews.com / www.lonniemathews.com

Five Financial Principles to Live By

Lonnie Mathews

Are you were you want be financially?

Truthfully, I have not always been the financial expert that I am today *(and I use the term "financial expert" loosely)*. I remember having financial problems early in life. Shortly after graduating college, my wife and I found ourselves neck deep in debt with horrible credit. This was partly because we didn't have a foundation of financial knowledge. In other words, we didn't live by any particular financial principles. Since then, we have discovered and lived by a set of financial principles that have transformed our lives. Today, I can honestly say that with each passing year, we are better off financially than we were the previous year.

This new way of thinking required us to make changes in our lifestyle. I was always uneasy about our financial situation. However, for a long time, I was not uncomfortable enough to do anything about it. I eventually developed a five step strategy that changed our financial future, and it can change yours too!

These principles are the foundation for a book called "Spend Everything". Before I reveal these principles to you, I must warn you that there are no big secrets involved. In fact, after you read them you might think to yourself, "that's nothing new, or I knew that already". If you knew this already, then why haven't you done anything about your situation?

The five principles that will revolutionize your financial future are:

- Think Net Worth
- Set Financial Goals
- Spend Less Than You Earn
- Save Regularly
- Reduce and Eliminate Debt

By implementing this five principle plan into your financial life, you will begin to see a change in your current situation. My wife and I have been living this plan for the past ten years, and our lives have not been the same since. At first glance, these concepts may seem simple. Sometimes, simple is the best option. People often ask, "Does this stuff really work?" My answer is always, "YES!" There are no shortcuts or secrets.

Think Net Worth –You must first understand what your net worth is. The basic accounting formula for determining net worth is: ASSETS – LIABILITIES = NET WORTH. Assets are the things that you own. Liabilities are the people that you owe. When deciding whether or not to make a large purchase, ask yourself: "Will purchasing this item increase or decrease my net worth?" If the answer is "decrease," then you must decide if it is worth it to purchase the item.

Set Financial Goals - Setting financial goals is a very important step in achieving financial freedom. Every successful person who has ever accomplished anything had to set some goals along the way. You must know where you want to go financially in order to get to where you want to be. This concept is so important that I have dedicated an entire section in my book to helping you set and achieve financial goals.

Spend Less Than You Earn - At first glance this may sound simple, but it has proven to be very difficult to accomplish. The concept of spending less than you earn requires you to re-introduce a word back into your vocabulary that most people have forgotten. That word is NO! In order to spend less than you earn, you must learn to say "no" more often. Let's practice. On the count of three, I want you to yell loudly and enthusiastically: No!

1 – 2 – 3 . . . NO!

No, I will not continue to spend more than I make! No, I will not continue to jeopardize my future by spending money that I do not currently have! No, I don't want to continue to live my life this way!

Save Regularly - The very thought of saving money has escaped our society. Recent statistics show that Americans have a negative saving rate. What? How can you have a negative saving rate? It's easy when you consider that most Americans spend $1.22 for every dollar that they earn. I once read a book called *The Richest Man in Babylon* by George S. Clauson, and it illustrated the story of the richest man in Babylon. Someone once asked how he became the richest man in Babylon, and his response was, "I learned early on that a tenth of all that I earn is mine to keep." In order to positively change your financial situation, you must save money on a regular basis.

Reduce and Eliminate Debt - To truly escape the past, you have to rid yourself of all payments from past decisions and start down a new path. Start down a path that does not include financing things that you really do not need. How would your life be different if you didn't have all the payments that you currently have? Imagine getting your paycheck and the only bills you had to pay were your everyday living expenses. What if you didn't have the car payment that you now have? What if you didn't have to make the minimum payment on those credit cards? What if you didn't have that student loan payment that you are still making payments on after having graduated from college ten years ago? In order to get where you want to be financially, you must develop a plan to reduce and eliminate all debt from your current financial life.

Remember to get where you want to be you do the things necessary to get you there. Don't go another year continuing to make the same financial mistakes. In order to change your financial situation, you must begin to think differently. Most importantly, you need to do something DIFFERENT!

Tony Gordon

Tony Gordon was born in Little Rock, Arkansas. He is a resident of Huntsville, Alabama. He is a graduate of Jacksonville State University, where he was a two sport athlete. Gordon, an avid fitness enthusiast, has been a world champion power lifter. He is also an author and playwright with several books to his credit. Gordon has a passion for community service and is shown by his mentoring and training of youth athletes. Several of whom have gone on to receive scholarships to play collegiately. He is an active volunteer and supporter with the Boy Scouts of America. He is a member of Phi Beta Sigma Fraternity, Inc.

Self Control, not Remote Control

Tony Gordon

When you google the definition of self-control, it reads "the ability to control oneself, in particular one's emotions and desires or the expression of them in one's behavior, especially in difficult situations."

Remote control is defined as the control of an activity, process, or machine from a distance, as by radioed instructions or coded signals.

I think self-control is one of the most profound but often under analyzed words in the English language. I feel that many people don't really have self-control. I feel that many people do not know that they lack self-control. There are times in a young man's life when they must give control to others. When you are a baby, you lack self-control and must have a parent to provide basic care to you such as eating, cleaning yourself, and clothing yourself. You need less help as you mature. You can cook, clean, dress yourself, and make minor decisions as a preteen. You can legally sign documents at the age of 18. At 21, you are considered a full-fledged adult with all rights and responsibilities.

Self-Control does not equal age, maturity, or education. Let me give some examples of what is not self-control.

1. You are age 17. You have a driver's license. You decide to race your new car on an old road because you were challenged by a rival. You are old enough and a legal driver but the rival has a remote control.
2. You are 21. It's your birthday. You go to a bar and your friends by you several rounds of drinks to celebrate but you don't drink. You drink because you have reached the legal drinking age. Your friends have the remote control and pushed the drink button.
3. You are 40 years old. You have dated the same person since college. Everyone says you should marry her, including her, because you are getting older and need to settle down. They hold the remote control on your idea of marriage.

In the above examples, all of the people did not display self-control. They did not control their own desires or emotions. The chose to allow external influences to dictate their actions. When you allow others to have a remote control to you, things can go drastically awry. The 17 year old could have crashed. The 21 year old could have drank too much and gotten sick or worse. The 40 year old could marry the person and soon end with a divorce and a destroyed friendship or friendships.

I cannot stress this enough to young men. DO NOT give people a remote control to your life. In order to achieve the true greatness that is within you, you must have self-control. You must be able to control yourself, your emotions, your desires, and the way you express them. Your elders mean well and have great intentions but do not always give you good advice. LeBron James and Allen Iverson were tremendous football players. At some point, I'm sure they were told to focus on football solely. What might have occurred if they didn't have self-control and listened to those people? Bill Gates was told that a GUI (Graphical User Interface) would never work. He did not allow his mentors and even peers detour his dreams. He did not give them the remote control. He built an operating system based on GUI's and Microsoft dominating the computing industry.

Many parents do a great job at setting the course for their children. They tell their kids that they could live the American dream if I they work hard. They tell you to get an education, get a job, get married, and have kids. This is because this is what they were taught. They were told to do just that and many did it. This is believed to be a successful and fulfilling existence. They really mean well. Many females are taught that a knight in shining armor will come to them and swoop them up. Others are taught that men are dogs and you should be cunning and smart to manipulate what you want from them. Males are taught that a real man has a family and takes care of them. They are taught to seek the most beautiful woman around and sweep her off her feet. These teachings and ideas become ingrained in our minds that this is what we are supposed to do. This makes us good citizens if we do this. What about self-control though? Was the typical so-called American dream our true desire? It could be. If it is not, then someone has a remote control that controls you.

What is a young man to do when everyone has some sort of input into his life? Pick the buttons that work for you. Everyone has a strength. Everyone has a weakness. Everyone has a true burning passion inside them that they want to do. Learn what your strengths are. You may be physically gifted. Play a sport if you are. You may be intellectually gifted. Use that talent to learn and consume as much information and knowledge as possible. You may be talented at communicating with people. Learn how to effectively communicate and improve that skill. The buttons you pick can change your course of life to something you could have never imagined. If someone pushes those buttons, they are steering that course.

Whatever your gift may be, the way to success is not necessarily hard work. It may be in you being able to be an innovator. Hard work does not always pay off. This is a fact. Do not let anyone tell you otherwise. Smart work does pay off.

If you have heard of the story of John Henry against the machine, then you know he beat the machine. I always hated that story because of its skewed message. You should always work hard and go that extra mile and you will be rewarded. Everyone was proud that John Henry beat the machine. John Henry however, was dead afterwards. He never got to enjoy his accomplishments. I see many people work hard for success but never enjoy the reward. Many never reach the level of success they desire. Some people reach success only to find out they are successful at something they really never liked. This can be a hurtful feeling. Kim K has worked smart at not working hard. She gets paid to do very little. She loves attention. This is her success. I am not telling you to be lazy. I am telling you to focus, plan, execute, then evaluate, your work. Most people say you have to work hard to accomplish something. They have been programmed to say this. Someone has a remote control on them. I liken these people to John Henry and his sledgehammer. John Henry only focused and executed his mission. He did not get to evaluate it because he died of exhaustion. Had he planned, maybe the outcome would have been different. So the lesson here is don't be John Henry. Be like John Lee Love. John Lee Love patented a portable pencil sharpener known as "the Love Sharpener." Be an innovator.

You only get one life. You only get one chance at this life to do it right. You may encounter roadblocks, defeats, and missteps along the way. This is why you must control your destiny. This is why you cannot give anyone a remote control to you. Parents, teachers, friends, coaches, mentors, girlfriends think they know what is best for you. You have to learn what is best for you. Do not give them the remote control. You have to learn then implement the true meaning of self-control. You have to have the ability to control your emotions and desires or the expression of them. Now go out there and change the world! That is if you desire to do that.

Steven G. Stewart

My name is Steven Stewart. I was born In Huntsville Alabama. I'm not one for accolades or titles simply because I have met a lot of programmed people with degrees and positions, who hold their status in high regard. If a man brings good energy and good overstanding, why waste time judging how he came to this conclusion or knowledge.

We were ostracized in this same manner, so it's a little disturbing to watch my people imitate this degenerative behavior. The Ab-original Black man could not get a job or hold positions simply because he did not hold a degree or certificate from his suppressor. In this day and time many Ab-original people have degrees and hold positions, and even though they don't really control anything to date they are proud of their accolades.

I'm going in like this because it should not be about me; it should be more about the message. Having said that, I hope that you can take something from this man's point of view... Hotep family

Hotep Family

Steven G. Stewart

I come from the one, just as you come from the one. If you take the light of the sun and focus it into a prism, you get many different variations of the one light. We are those variations; though we have been programmed to think otherwise. The devil was cast out of heaven because of pride. You have been indoctrinated to be proud. "Proud to be an American" "I'm black and I'm proud" "I'm so proud of you. Why can't we be proud to be a part of the one? "I'm the best" "I did that" "what about me"...etc. I find it interesting that we and our children have been subtly taught to feel and think this way.

I was asked to write on a specific subject or title. In preparing to do so, it dawned on me that this subject is multilayered. My interpretation of, "my now for the future man" started as me seeing myself as now and my 9 year old son as the future man or metaphysically speaking "me". Yet I also see it as, the generation from 10,000 years ago, as the now, and this generation as the future generation. I'd like to speak on the former first and then the latter.

My son is a remarkable young man. I have never spoken to him as if he were a child. I have always spoken to him as if he is an adult and can understand. I have long since recognized that he is me and I AM he. I give him as much information as I can, in a delicate manner of course. It has taken me many years to acquire the knowledge that exists in my brain. I have had to turn over a thousand rocks to find one Gem. I would like to show my future man, which rocks to look under for the same Gems. In doing so he will save time looking, and can use the same time to create, to perpetuate our line, our species into the future.

I won't have enough time to cover all the things that go with this subject here, so please forgive me for the condensation of this pertinent information.

The first thing that we must be able to see, to even grasp the gravity of this topic, is the whole picture. You don't have to understand, but you must know that it exist, and is real.

The Ab-original man or Asiatic black man, from Kemet or "the land of the black", has been a victim of a most sinister plot. You have been taught his-story but not how it correlates to you. We were first; wait let me repeat that, WE WERE FIRST. They looked long and hard for a new country. (Christopher Columbus, Amerigo Vespucci. Leif Erikson...etc.) In those days this would have taken a lot of time and resources, seeing that there were no satellites, no computers, no real maps and no communication. In a time where they believed that the world was flat, they chose to voyage into the unknown, for what must have been a great purpose. They sent mission after mission to find a new country, but why? What was wrong with their land/country, or was it something else. Once they acquired the land they needed someone to build structures to cultivate the land. They found Hiram abiff....hit him in the head and drug him on a north westerly course and buried him in a shallow grave. In order to make the slaves subservient they began the first forms of psychological warfare on them. (The dry bones in the valley) Some of these forms manifested as rape, murder, and splitting the families up (chattel slavery) hanging a pregnant woman upside down cutting the belly till the baby fell out then stomped it to death while they made the other slaves watch. Refusing to let you read, write or worship your own higher power. Anything African has always been demonized...In spite of all his efforts the whole world still wants to be like you. While you still want to be like him. The Ab-original man in America is the only man that will adopt something that is not of him. Go into any other society/community; the Koreans know their language and have a Korean image of their god. China town, they know their language and have a Chinese image of their god. The Caucasian has his own language that he derived from you, as everything that he does, he derives it from you. His image of god is Caucasian... People of color outside of Africa have no language and have a white image of god. We wouldn't dare practice our own religion. I digress. They found a country, found a man that could build anything, and begin to build a blank man. This plot has been going on for more than 500 yrs. now. This is of course a condensed version, so bear with me, but looking at it this way you should have a better understanding of what's to come.

My now for the future man. My son has features like me, mentally and physically. What solidified this concept for me? When I'm frustrated, or having a problem, he can sense it. It doesn't matter what he's doing he focuses on me, assesses the problem then gives me advice. To my surprise he's right more times than he is wrong... Metaphysically it makes sense he is closer to God than I, so his solutions are not tainted by time on this hellish plane. I used to cut him off by saying, "go play" or "this is grown up stuff you wouldn't understand". Suffice it to say, I look forward to his advice now. To my future self, I'd say, stand strong because you were designed that way. Always listen to your inner self, because that is where you find God, not by following some phony religion. You should read as much as possible. There are 3 stories that come to mind. There are many more profound stories, but what better way to understand, than to read it straight from the opposition. The conflict between Cain and Able, the conflict between Esau and Jacob, and the story of Joseph. The first two represent the two major groups on the planet and one has always tried to steal the birthright of the other.(people of color and recessive people) If you forget, or allow the past to be erased., once you pass away the future will be high jacked. The same way that we are talking about my now for the future man, it can be used to erase the future man......over stand. The story of Joseph shows that as long as you hold true to the God within you, you will always succeed. "I AM" "Alpha and Omega" "I'm the first and the last".

When it comes to race you should never hate, but always perceive and understand. The gazelle doesn't hate the lion, but he does understand the nature of the lion. You won't find a gazelle trying to be friends with the lion, or buying food form the lion, or when he gets sick he goes to the lion. While I'm on animals, nature is the most important aspect of life. It is the textbook of life. If you take all the animals, insects, birds and fish and put them all together then you get man, or should I say woman, who then created man. Each entity on this planet is a part of you. To know them is to know yourself.

Speaking of woman. This subject would easily fit into volumes of books. She is the closest thing to God on this planet. I'll take a brief moment for you disbelievers, you male chauvinist... She has attraction powers on the planet and the moon. She has 15% more genetic material than the man. She decides the gender of the baby, not the man as you were taught. Let me show you in math. If the most high is represented by 0 (being the omnipotent objective force) for him to know himself he experiences himself through his creations the first was 1 or an odd, or woman. The next creation which came from woman was 2. Now think why would the most high create man then create woman, when he could create woman and have her follow her nature and create man.....think. Woman or the feminine principle is the only one on the planet capable of reproduction. For the sake of this subject, when we add we take two or more things already created and put them together. When we multiply we take one thing (sperm) and produce two from one, or three from one...etc. in light of this, woman is 1 or odd, or negative if you will...and before you women start with me please understand that terms are relative... now take the odd number and multiply it 1x1=1 1x2=2 1x3=3 1x4=4. Notice how the outcome goes from odd first then even then odd...etc. This means that the odd number has the potential to produce both, as with nature. Next let's look at the even or positive. 2x1=2 2x2=4 2x3=6 2x4=8, notice how 2 can only produce an even or positive or a male...just like in nature. He only has an XY set of chromosomes. If you add 15% more or another small line to the Y chromosome he would have xx...think. She is the creator, the nurturer etc. Take the word Neter, the Kemetic word for the most high. Neter or Nature, Mother Neter or Mother Nature. Without woman no man would be here, for we all came out of the wormhole or womb or sacred temple that exist between her legs. So protect your woman, all women. Protect her from disruptive ideas, from alien men; she is the foundation of civilization. She is so valuable, that when we were slaves, the slaves master would use her to nurse his own baby. That is how much he believed in the Black woman. Because the link was broken, we were taught to disrespect our black woman, to lust after her. We were taught to put the full burden on her. We were taught to fuck instead of make love to her. This was psychological warfare on her as well (the black woman) we participate in it, but it wasn't our design. The purpose was to show the world and the black woman, that she doesn't need us (black man), she needs him. Keep your eyes on the prize or lose it. If you lose her than you are nothing.

The whole world will be taught to hate you. Every civilization will look down upon you, in spite of your contributions to the world. Whenever you are made to feel this way, just remember that you are the sun/son of god. When comparing you to the black woman you pale slightly, but when compared to any other race, you exceed all limits. Never let anyone dictate your worth. Work for yourself, grow your own food, and when you get sick, pick herbs. That way you will know what is in your medicine. Last but not least Blackman; meditate, meditate, meditate. This is where true knowledge comes from, and don't spend a lot of time trying to convince people of what you know. Spend time practicing what you know, and by doing so everyone will follow you.

I won't spend as much time on "My Generation for the future Generation" For the information would seem redundant. Through the last Golden age we laid, and by we, I mean the Ab-original Black man of the planet; we laid a foundation that would last and stand as the foundation of the next Golden age. We are currently embarking on a new Golden age. Which begins in 2020. The last one was 10 -10 thousand years ago. During this time the black masters built pyramids, and intertwined them with hieroglyphs, metaphysics, astrology, math, agriculture, science, magic, harmonics, Nano technology, macro and micro technology, future and past stories. While you were taught that Kemet (Egypt) was a place of heathens that worship hundreds of gods. They have been raping and dissecting our motherland for centuries. There have been more books written about Egypt than all other subjects put together. As I close let me say that we have been doing this forever, just as the animals do.

A shark builds on each generation, over and over. It doesn't break the cycle to become famous, or to be CEO. It doesn't let the octopus baby sit its children, while it becomes professional. The cycle that we are on is a great grand cycle and it takes a proficient individual to grasp the concept. There are pyramids all over the earth, and they all have a story to tell that mimics one another. They stand as a beacon for a time when consciousness sparks again, as the seed does. The new generation of the new Golden age can begin to rebuild on what's been left. So this topic to me serves the same point. When my 9 year old becomes a man, when his conscience sparks he can read these words and get a basic understanding of life's format. If he does the same for his future man, then 2000 years from now this chapter may be just as deep if not deeper than the pyramid text of Kemet, Asia, Korea, Japan, China, North America, South America North pole, Europe...etc. We built structures everywhere. We left chapters all over the earth. We knew and understood that in order to have day you must allow for the night. In order to have summer we must allow for the winter. In order to have birth you must allow for death. We are about to be born again metaphysically. The All, The One consciousness is about to be reborn. All existence is based on opposites and attraction, light and sound.....Peace family.

Love has no past Love has no future

Love has no past; all of our experiences that live in the past, we classify them as memories. We grow and learn from our memories. If we love the past or love in the past, it's probably because we are afraid of the present. (Of what could be)

Love has no past; because if it did, it would contradict itself. I can't love in the past, because love is a verb, it moves, it is an action. If it were to stop, stagnate or lie dormant, it becomes something else; a memory, past tense. Love is action, or should i say my actions, and I can only act today, right now. Yesterday is gone and tomorrow might not come. So today I will love with every atom of my essence. It (Love) will show in my actions. "I love you" this is merely a phrase. When you put forth good wholesome actions... that is love. Anything else would have to be a memory of love, or the hope of finding Love.

Love has no future; things that live and exist in the future, we call them ideas or dreams. Love has no future, because in order to make it to the future, there must be a present a now, a time when action takes place. Love has no past, nor does it have a future, because it exists in the moment.

We reflect on the past in order to over stand that we must learn to love more in the future. And once we learn to love, we begin to embrace love and the effects that love has on us. Then we look to the future hoping to hold on to this everyday action, this illustrious manifestation of the true essence within.....LOVE.

Sharon A. Myers

Sharon A. Myers is the Founder and CEO of Moovin4ward Presentations, an empowerment company that facilitates leadership development, and entrepreneurial programs for youth, students and professionals. She is the developer of several youth programs to include **Journey to Success: Personal Success Strategic Plan (PSSP) Program**, which is based on the book *Mapping Your Journey to Success: Six Steps for Personal Planning*. She has also developed the **My Now Career & Leadership Conference** and the **Young Entrepreneur Success (YES!) Program**.

sharon@moovin4ward.com
www.Moovin4ward.com
www.Moovin4wardTraining.com
www.Journey2SuccessPSSP.com
www.MyNowBooks.com
Tweet @moovin4ward

The First Lady

Sharon A. Myers

It's no secret that mothers and sons have a distinctive bond. I've been blessed to have two sons and two daughters. I can truly say that I love all of them equally, but I have special connections with my sons.

As a whole, this book is all about helping you to become a "responsible, accountable, and respectable" man, learning to understand and be the best you that you can be in all areas of life. It includes the guidance and wisdom of great men from around the country—men who are successful businessmen, fathers, sons, boyfriends or husbands.

My contribution, as the only female contributor, comes from a woman's perspective. I predict that as you get older and become wiser you will know to cherish the relationships you have with "special" women. But I want to talk a moment about the *most* special lady, your FIRST lady... your mother.

Mama's Boy

It's been said that "It takes a man to raise a man." I don't disagree with this theory at all. I think it is absolutely necessary for you to have access to positive male role models throughout every stage of your life cycle, especially your father. But I also believe that the relationship that you have with your mother is also very necessary.

Mothers have been told since forever, to not "baby" our sons or it will prevent them from growing up to be strong, independent men. We have been told that if we keep our sons too close to us, we will damage his manhood and create wimpy, dependent "mama's boys." This may have more to do with the personality types of the mother and the son than it does with just "over mothering." And let's be honest, separating a boy from the nurturing of his mother *prematurely*, and forcing him to "man up" can be equally damaging.

Fathers tend to build relationships with their sons by "doing stuff" with them—actively playing with them. For mothers, the process for building a relationship may be a bit different. There are a few of us who also actively play with our sons (neither of mine could stop my 3 point shot); but in most cases, our relationship with our sons grow by simply "being there." Many young men will say that their mom is that one person who truly gets them AND accepts them for who they are. Don't get me wrong, there may be some who have a similar relationship with their fathers... but most young men want to be strong for their fathers, so they may or may not be willing to show any weakness. That's not necessary with their *first lady.*

If your relationship with your mother is healthy, your bond with your mother will be one of the deepest, most enduring relationships you will experience in your lifetime. It can also be a precursor to the relationships you will have with women. It's been said that when young man's relationship with his mother is healthy and supporting, he will likely:

Be less hostile. Young men with strong, secure and positive relationships with their mothers tend to be less destructive and aggressive, therefore less prone to delinquency and/or to be challenging in macho proving activities.

Be more expressive. Mothers tend to nurture emotional intelligence in their sons, teaching them to recognize and express their own feelings and to be more attuned to the feelings of others. This contributes to the having better self-control of their actions and empathy for others.

Be more communicative. Mothers tend to encourage their sons to talk more when sharing a thought or opinion, and are less likely to accept grunts and moans as conversation. This can contribute to young men being more articulate and better conversationalists.

Be less precarious. It has long been known that good parent-teen communication can help lessen the influence of negative peer pressure. While many fathers are waiting for a certain age or maturity to have "the talk", mothers are weaving in the difficult topics into everyday activities and discussions.

These very same skills can be carried into the workplace. Once upon a time, it was thought that a brute physical strength and a dominating style were the tickets to success. Not anymore. Today, you need the ability to work in teams and to have the communications and social intelligence skills that your mother has been teaching you all along.

These skills can also be carried into your relationships. These days, communicative women aren't attracted to the "strong silent type" and the guy who has a habit of punching holes in walls to express anger is not appealing at all. Women are being taught to recognize, appreciate and pursue the guy who genuinely respects and loves his mother, because this guy will know how to respect and love his mate.

The Grand Lady

"There is nothing more attractive to a woman than a man who adores his mom, treats her well, treats her with respect and goes out of his way to help her. There is also nothing more unattractive to a woman than a man who can't stand up to

his mother, who lets his mother control him, who fears his mother and who puts his mommy first" - Jackie Pilossoph.

At some point in your life, your mother may no longer be your first lady. But this can't and won't happen overnight. When you fall in love with the woman of your dreams, your mother may need time to transition from her First Lady position. There will probably be some tension or jealousy. But it will be your responsibility to make sure that she understands that she's not being moved out, but elevated up... to Grand Lady. And although a serious girlfriend or wife may recognize the benefit of your mother's good influence, she may also be opposed to the mother's continued role in your life. If at any point you feel caught in the middle, don't withdraw from the battle field. No one wins if you go missing or become a prisoner of war.

Many men don't know what kind of relationship to have with their mothers after they engage in a serious relationship. There are numerous life circumstances that contribute to the connection between a mother and son. Perhaps his father left when he was a child and his mother was all he had. Perhaps his father died and he feels obligated to compensate for her loss. Or perhaps his father treated his mother cruelly, and he feels the need to protect her.

While these are all admirable justifications to treat your mother as the Queen that she is, be sure that you maintain a relationship with her that's healthy for *both* of you. Here are a few tips to consider:

Mandatory versus Voluntary

You should never feel it "mandatory" to spend time with your mother and/or put her ahead of your own plans. Unless there's an emergency, repeatedly dropping everything to respond when she calls or summons will cause major issues with your mate. Instead, learn to draw the line and let your mother know that you are unavailable. Then consider finding time to reach out to and/or make plans to hang out with her when you *are* free. Be sure to remind her how much you love her.

Anxiety versus Honesty

Being anxious over whether you will anger or disappoint your mother because you don't do everything she asks, *immediately* when she asks, *should* go away with adulthood. In a healthy relationship with your mother, you understand that she loves you unconditionally and not just when you please her. If you respond to your mother's every whim out of fear, you will undoubtedly frustrate your mate. Chances are slim that you will live a full life and *never* disappoint her. Your best bet is to be upfront and completely honest... she'll eventually get over it.

Bitterness versus Happiness

You know that you have a great relationship with your mother when you get a joy out of seeing her every time you get together. You grow to truly cherish those moments of laughter, reminiscing or having those deep personal discussions. If you are dreading what should be happy times with her, then there are some issues that need to be resolved. If those issues are allowed to remain out of fear, you will become more annoyed and possibly angry with yourself for being annoyed. It will just be a matter of time before this bitterness flows into your relationship with your mate.

In Closing

You should always treat your mother with kindness, respect and gratitude. That's a given. She will always be your first lady. But you should do this because you WANT to, not because she expects you to. As you become a man, remember to continue to maintain the best relationship you can with your mother. A solid relationship with your mother can contribute to your career success AND is a good sign for a healthy love relationships. Also understand that you are to be the facilitator of a great relationship between your First Lady and the lady who will succeed her. Ensure that the relationship between them is equally as good... especially as your mother transitions from the First Lady to the Grand Lady.

My Now...

Books by Moovin4ward Publishing

My Now for the Student Leader
Motivation to Develop and Improve Leadership Skills

By Moovin4ward Authors

My Now for the Single Parent
Motivation to Be The Best Parent Regardless of Marital Status

By Moovin4ward Authors

My Now for the College Grad:
Motivation to Succeed After College

By Moovin4ward Authors

My Now for the Entrepreneur: Motivation to Start Your Own Business

By Moovin4ward Authors

My Vision, My Plan, MY NOW: Motivation You Need to Take the Action You Want

By Moovin4ward Authors

Mapping Your Journey to Success: Six Strategies for Personal Success

By Sharon A. Myers & Mark W. Wiggins

To book a certified Moovin4ward author to speak at an event email speakers@moovin4ward.com

To purchase Moovin4ward books in bulk (20+) at discounted rates, email books@moovin4ward.com.

www.Moovin4ward.com or www.MyNowBooks.com.